Retold Myths & Folktales

African Myths

African American Folktales

Asian Myths

Classic Myths, Volume 1

Classic Myths, Volume 2

Classic Myths, Volume 3

Mexican American Folktales

Native American Myths

Northern European Myths

World Myths

The Retold Tales® Series features novels, short story anthologies, and collections of myths and folktales.

Perfection Learning®

Reviewers

Rekha Basu
Des Moines, Iowa

Florence Hongo
San Mateo, California

Dr. Song Hu
Des Moines, Iowa

Father Tan Von Tran
Des Moines, Iowa

Retold Myths & Folktales

Asian Myths

by Frederick Y. Lagbao

Perfection Learning®

Written by
Frederick Y. Lagbao
Radio broadcaster/storyteller
Manila, Philippines

Senior Editor
Marsha James

Editor
Lisa Morlock

Cover and Inside Illustration
Donald E. Tate II

Book Design
Sue Bjork

For information contact
Perfection Learning® Corporation
1000 North Second Avenue, P.O. Box 500
Logan, Iowa 51546-0500
Phone: 1-800-831-4190 • Fax: 1-800-543-2745
Reinforced Library Binding ISBN-13: 978-0-7807-6575-7
Reinforced Library Binding ISBN-10: 0-7807-6575-3
Paperback ISBN-13: 978-0-7891-1894-3
Paperback ISBN-10: 0-7891-1894-7
PPI / 02 / 12
12 13 14 15 16 PP 17 16 15 14 13 12
perfectionlearning.com

TABLE

OF CONTENTS

WELCOME

MAP OF ASIA

WELCOME TO THE RETOLD ASIAN MYTHS AND FOLKTALES

Imagine a story that is so interesting that it's retold for thousands of years! Visualize children sitting around a storyteller and listening to this tale. Then visualize those same listeners as adults retelling the story to other children. This is how the oral tradition of storytelling keeps myths and folktales alive in Asia and other continents around the globe.

Not only are these stories entertaining to the audience, they are educational as well. Listeners can learn such things as how to behave, how to treat others, and how the Milky Way was formed.

The stories in this book are from several Asian countries. Asia is the largest continent in the world. It is as rich in history as it is dense with people. Over sixty percent of the world's population live in mainland Asia and its islands. As the map shows, Asian countries include China, India, Thailand, Cambodia, Laos, Vietnam, Japan, Korea, and the Philippine Islands. With so many people spread over such a large area, it's easy to understand why Asia is a rainbow of cultures and races.

Asia is also a mixture of religions. The major religions are Hinduism, Buddhism, and Taoism. You'll read myths in this book that reflect the beliefs of these religions and others.

From reading myths, we can learn a lot about people and their cultures. Myths provide insights into parts of a culture that a textbook can't cover.

RETOLD UPDATE

Each of the fifteen stories in this book has been carefully chosen to help you learn something about a cultural group from Asia. They give you a picture of the past, as well as an understanding of the world you live in today.

The myths in this book have been retold once again— this time in written form. As you read each myth, imagine how a storyteller would have presented it. What types of movements might have been incorporated with the words? What sounds or vocal tones might have been added? Try to actually hear the story being told to you.

Since these myths are written down, several features have been added to help you interact with the story. Challenging words and their definitions are listed at the beginning of each story. These words are boldfaced within the story. If you forget the meaning of a word as you read, just check the list to review the definition.

You'll also see footnotes at the bottom of some pages. These notes identify people or places, explain ideas or words, or give you the pronunciation of unfamiliar words. The map will help you place each story in its geographical location. This will help you visualize where each story originated.

Remember, the stories in this book are only one version of stories told all over the world for hundreds of years by hundreds of different storytellers. You might know similar versions of these retold stories. This is not unusual. You may even wish to retell one of these stories in your own style. In this way, you can continue to give life to these ageless tales.

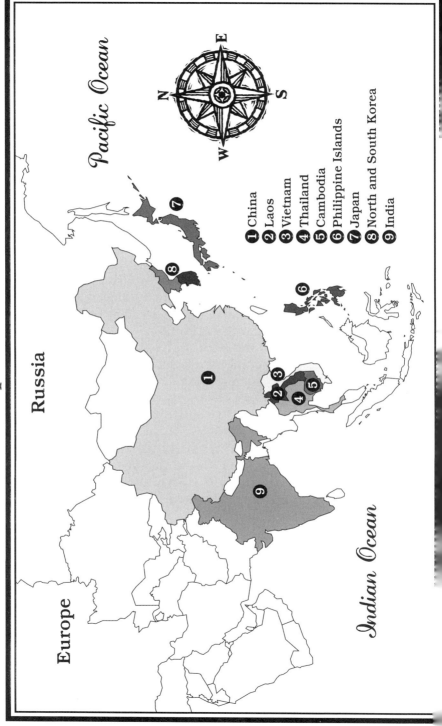

Map of Asia

Pacific Ocean

Russia

Europe

Indian Ocean

❶ China
❷ Laos
❸ Vietnam
❹ Thailand
❺ Cambodia
❻ Philippine Islands
❼ Japan
❽ North and South Korea
❾ India

A · S · I · A · N

GODS AND HUMANS

The Tree of Life

Wish for Power

The Lucky Straw

Religion is deeply rooted in the Asian culture. Followers of Eastern religions look to several gods and goddesses for spiritual guidance. Tales of these deities have been retold for generations. Listeners learn valuable lessons about life from these stories.

The myths in this section reveal struggles between gods and humans, as well as struggles between the gods themselves. Notice the lessons each myth teaches the reader or listener in the original telling.

M · Y · T · H · S

THE TREE OF LIFE

VOCABULARY PREVIEW

The following words appear in the story. Review the list and get to know the words before you read the story.

churning—heaving; tossing
domain—kingdom; territory
extracted—drew out
hesitation—delay; waiting
husked—peeled; skinned
impostor—fake; pretender
lamenting—grieving; mourning
lava—burning rock that flows from a volcano's eruption
mortals—humans; beings able to die
nourishment—food; nutrition
petty—little; foolish
pondering—thinking; reviewing
rival—competitor; enemy
spewing—spitting; throwing
surge—flow; rush
waning—weakening; tiring

Main Characters

Bathala—god of the land
Dagatkalulua—god of the oceans and seas
Galangkalulua—god of the sky

In the beginning, the earth consisted only of rocks and dirt. One day the god of the land was lonely, so he decided to make humans. Only it wasn't as simple as he'd thought.

The Tree of Life

Adapted from a Filipino tale

In the beginning, there were three gods in the universe: the god of the land, the god of the oceans and seas, and the god of the sky. But oddly enough, each god thought that he was the only one who existed.

Bathala,[1] the god of the land, was a mighty giant. He looked just like you and me, except that he was much larger.

One day Bathala said to himself, "It is a fine thing to be the ruler of the universe, but for some reason I am not happy. Maybe it is because I am all alone. Life would be more interesting if only I had some beings as smart and

[1] (bät hä´ la)

interesting as I am to keep me company. Perhaps I could create some **mortals**."

Bathala smiled as he imagined how pleasant it would be to share the land with humans. Of course, he would not make these creatures exactly like himself. He would make them mortal so that each would have an interesting life story with a beginning, a middle, and an end. And he would make the creatures small so there would be room on the land for them to multiply.

But then as he looked around at the barren, rocky ground, his smile faded. Nothing grew anywhere on the land. "Humans need food and shelter," he thought. "Where will they find either on these lifeless plains? I must give this problem some serious thought!"

He sat down on a cliff overlooking the vast ocean. With his knees hugged to his chest and his forehead resting on his knees, he looked like a big egg-shaped rock balanced on the top of the cliff.

As Bathala was **pondering** this problem, Dagatkalulua[2] swam by. Dagatkalulua was a huge, scaly serpent god who ruled the oceans and seas. He swam through the water by coiling and uncoiling his body with powerful thrusts that sent huge waves crashing toward shore. As he swam, he raised his long, curved neck so his flat head swayed above the water.

Dagatkalulua caught a glimpse of Bathala out of the corner of his eye, and the two gods stared at each other in astonishment. Then Dagatkalulua called out, "You, there! Who are you?"

"I am Bathala, the ruler of the universe."

"Ha, do not make me laugh!" answered Dagatkalulua rudely. "You cannot be the ruler of the universe. I am."

"Liar!" cried the giant, shaking his huge fist. "I am the ruler, and I'll twist your neck to prove it!"

"**Impostor**!" shouted the sea serpent, baring hundreds of sharp, pointed teeth. "I am the ruler, and I'll bite your head off to prove it!"

---

[2] (dä gät´ kə lü´ lü ə) Dagatkalulua means "soul of the sea."

There was a pause while each searched his mind for another threat. "Well," said Bathala after a moment, "since you will not listen to reason, I'll just have to beat the truth into you."

"Go ahead and try it," answered Dagatkalulua as he rushed toward Bathala. "But when your hair turns to seaweed, don't say I didn't warn you."

Bathala swerved out of the way as Dagatkalulua stretched his long neck to strike Bathala off his high cliff. Bathala shouted back, "That was a **petty** show of your so-called strength. You will be easy to destroy."

With that, Bathala hurled himself into Dagatkalulua's watery **domain**. Bathala attempted to choke the life from his **rival**, who was caught by surprise. However, with a mighty grunt Dagatkalulua threw Bathala farther from the shore. Without **hesitation**, Bathala swam toward Dagatkalulua, and the gods attacked each other again, thrashing about in the water. Their struggle sent the currents **churning** to shore. Great tidal waves flooded shorelines throughout the land. The battle raged for three days and three nights. The whole universe shook and shuddered while the two gods pounded each other.

As the battle continued into the fourth day, Bathala realized that his strength was **waning**. However, Dagatkalulua's seemed to be increasing. "I will never defeat him here, in his natural element," Bathala thought. "I must get him out of the water and onto the land."

Slowly Bathala retreated toward the shore. Dagatkalulua, thinking the giant was trying to escape, pursued him. The great struggle continued until they reached a place where Bathala could stand up. Immediately Bathala felt power from the earth **surge** through his body. Bathala lifted Dagatkalulua overhead and hurled the serpent onto the dry land. The sea serpent's great body landed with such force that huge jagged cracks appeared in the earth's surface. Fiery volcanoes **spewing** hot **lava** erupted from these openings.

But Dagatkalulua wasn't finished yet. With one last effort, he gave Bathala such a lashing with his whip-like tail that great howling hurricanes were created. Dagatkalulua lay motionless. At last the long battle was over. Just then Bathala realized what he had done. He had killed the only other living creature he'd ever known. Bathala knelt beside his dying opponent, and his heart filled with regret. With his last bit of strength, Bathala dug a grave in the stony soil and buried his rival. Then he lay down to rest and to wait for his injuries to heal.

Bathala recovered from his wounds, but he was even more lonely than before. "Dagatkalulua must have ruled the ocean," thought Bathala. "That means I only rule the land. I should not have gotten so angry when Dagatkalulua told me he was a god. If I could have controlled my pride, I could have made friends with him. Then I wouldn't be so lonely."

Now more than ever, Bathala realized how alone he was. Because of his quick temper, he had ruined a chance at friendship. And he still didn't have a plan for creating humans.

Several years passed. One day a strange being flew into Bathala's domain. It had a round head with lidless eyes, a flat nose, and a circular mouth. Two great wings were fastened to the sides of his head.

"You, there! Who are you?" called out Bathala.

"Hello there. I am Galangkalulua,[3] ruler of the skies," the newcomer said as he swooped past Bathala.

Remembering the mistakes he had made upon meeting Dagatkalulua, the giant greeted the newcomer politely. "I am Bathala, the ruler of the land," he said. "Welcome to my kingdom."

"Thank you," replied the other as he landed near Bathala. "I had always thought I was alone."

The giant answered, "I had always thought the same until one day I met a god named Dagatkalulua, the ruler of the oceans and seas."

[3] (gä´ läng kə lü´ lü ə) Galangkalulua means "soul of respect."

"There are three of us, then. That's wonderful!"

"Actually," said Bathala, "Dagatkalulua is gone. Would you like to know what happened?"

"Of course!" said Galangkalulua. "I am curious to know the story."

So Bathala told his guest about his battle with the sea god. He also spoke about his loneliness. And he talked of his desire to create people to live with him. He explained how the only obstacle was the harshness of the land.

Galangkalulua listened sympathetically. Then, in turn, he told Bathala about his life in the skies. The two agreed that it was a pleasure to have someone to talk to. They became good friends and enjoyed each other's company for many years.

Then one day, Galangkalulua became gravely ill. Bathala did everything he could to save his friend, but Galangkalulua grew weaker every day. It was clear that the god of the skies would not live much longer. Galangkalulua called Bathala to his side.

"My dear friend, I must soon leave you," he said. "But I do not wish to leave you all alone. Often you have told me that if your land were not so harsh, you would create humans to share the earth with you."

Bathala just nodded. His thoughts were full of concern for his friend.

Galangkalulua's voice sank to a whisper. "When I die, bury me in the same spot where you buried Dagatkalulua. From there I will give you the answer to your problem."

A few moments later, Galangkalulua died. Bathala let out a mournful cry, then retreated to his deepest cave.

After a day of **lamenting**, he remembered his promise to Galangkalulua. Bathala did what his friend had asked and buried Galangkalulua near Dagatkalulua. All the while, Bathala wept over the grave.

When his tears hit the ground, they seemed to soak deep into the earth. Just as Bathala finished covering the grave, a tree sprang up. It was a tall tree with a trunk that was shaped like Dagatkalulua's neck. It was also rough, like the scales of the dead sea god. The leaves, on the other hand, resembled the mighty wings of Galangkalulua. The tree produced a hard, round fruit. When Bathala **husked** the fruit, he saw that it looked like the head of his dead friend. It had two eyes, a flat nose, and a round mouth.

Suddenly Bathala realized that this tree was the answer that Galangkalulua had promised him. It was the Tree of Life. Now Bathala could populate the earth, knowing that this gift could give humans everything they needed to survive.

So Bathala created the first man and woman. The mortals built their house from the tree. Using the sturdy trunk as the walls, they made a thatched roof with the leaves. Later they discovered many more uses for the tree. The tree's soft, white meat and milky liquid offered **nourishment**. Oil from the dried meat was **extracted** for cooking. The leaves were used to make hats, mats, baskets, brooms, and furniture. The fiber from the leaves was made into rope. The tree gave people all they needed to live. And it continues to give life today.

Today we call it the coconut tree. But its true name is the one Bathala gave it—the Tree of Life.

INSIGHTS

"The Tree of Life" is a creation myth from the Philippine Islands, a Southeast Asian country. The country is inhabited by people of many different cultures. The original inhabitants of the islands, the Aetas,[1] were influenced by the Malays and the Indonesians. Later on, the cultural mix was enriched by the coming of the Chinese, Spanish, Japanese, and Americans.

There are other creation tales from the Philippines. One such tale describes the creation of the Philippine Islands. According to this legend, there was once a crow who couldn't find a place to land.

As he thought about his problem, he remembered an unusual incident he'd witnessed during one of his flights. It seems the sky and the ocean had a serious disagreement. In fact, the sky become so angry with the ocean that it swept up rocks from the mountains and pelted them into the water. The ocean answered back by spouting water at the sky. So many rocks were thrown into the angry water that an island was soon created.

Remembering this, the crow provoked an argument between the ocean and the sky. The crow told each of them that the other claimed to be more powerful. The trick worked. The ocean spewed water upward, while the sky hurled large rocks down. It was these rocks that eventually formed the more than seven thousand islands of the Philippines.

Bathala also appears in other variations of Philippine creation stories. In one, Bathala weeps because of his loneliness. His two teardrops become birds who ask for a place to roost, and Bathala creates the earth for them.

---

[1] (ē′ tas) The Aetas are a dark-skinned, pygmy-like people who probably migrated to the Philippines from the Malay Peninsula.

One of the birds hears a voice pleading for freedom from inside a large bamboo pole. The bird pecks at the bamboo until the pole splits open to reveal *Malakas*,[2] the first man on earth. The other bird hears a voice from inside another bamboo pole. It pecks at the second pole until it splits, and *Maganda*[3] emerges as the first woman on earth.

---

[2] (mä lä käs´) *Malakas* means strong.
[3] (mä gän dä´) *Maganda* means beautiful.

WISH FOR POWER

VOCABULARY PREVIEW

The following words appear in the story. Review the list and get to know the words before you read the story.

attire—clothing; apparel
awestruck—speechless; amazed
bedecked—decorated; trimmed
envious—jealous; discontented
escorting—guarding; attending
gaping—open; wide; large
impudence—boldness; rudeness
procession—parade; display
profusely—without limits; excessively
reflected—thought; considered
relished—enjoyed; delighted in
spectacle—show; wonder
strutting—parading; showing off; walking proudly
stupendous—greatest; exceptional
survey—look over; examine
trivial—small; not worth mentioning

Main Character

stonecutter—skillful and honorable common man

Be careful what you wish for because it might come true. A poor stonecutter learns this lesson. After many wishes, he discovers what makes him truly happy.

Wish for Power

Adapted from a Chinese folktale

There was once a stonecutter who was known for his skill at carving statues. He took pride in his work, and he earned enough money to pay for all the things in life he really needed. His home was simple, and there was always food on the table. He enjoyed the respect of his customers and the good will of his neighbors. In short, he lived an honorable and pleasant life.

Yet the stonecutter was not content. One evening as he finished a grand statue of Ts'ai Shen,[1] the God of Wealth, he felt very tired. Laying down his hammer and chisel, he stepped back to **survey** the work.

"This is my best creation yet. It looks just like the god," he said. He was pleased with the statue, but still he was not happy.

---

[1] (tsahy´ shen) Ts'ai Shen is a Taoist god. The religion of Taoism teaches that a long life is attained through simplicity and peace.

"Tomorrow I will deliver this fine statue to the temple priests," the stonecutter grumbled. "But instead of giving me the riches I deserve, I will be paid my usual **trivial** wage. The life of a poor man is filled with hard work and despair. Oh, how I wish I were a rich man instead!"

The next morning when the stonecutter went into his workshop, he stared in amazement at what he saw. The statue he had created was **bedecked** with dozens of necklaces, bracelets, and rings, all made of gold and precious gems. The God of Wealth had heard his prayer!

"Now that I am a rich man, I must live in a grand house," he declared. So he took the jewels to the village and sold them. Then he bought the finest building materials available and hired the most skilled carpenters. He ordered the workers to tear down his old hut and build a two-story mansion in its place.

But after the mansion was done, the stonecutter was still not satisfied. "How can I live in such a beautiful mansion in my tattered old clothes? I must buy new clothing," he said. So the stonecutter bought the most splendid clothing he could find.

Then he decided, "Now that I wear such lovely clothes, I can't possibly keep up this mansion by myself. I would get dirty." And so he hired many servants.

The stonecutter's life was filled with such good fortune that some of his neighbors became **envious** and resentful of him. They remembered him when he lived a peasant's life. However, the stonecutter was too busy enjoying his wealth to care what others thought of him.

One day he was strolling through the village when there was a sudden flurry of activity. Shopkeepers and peasants struggled to move to the side of the road.

"What's all this excitement about?" the stonecutter asked a peasant.

"Don't you know?" sputtered the peasant. "The mandarin[2] is coming! We must clear the way for his **procession**. Make haste to ready for his arrival." The peasant pushed his way to the side of the road.

[2] (man´ də rən) A *mandarin* is a high-ranking Chinese government official.

The mandarin's arrival was quite a **spectacle**. Servants carried him in a sedan,[3] and armed guards surrounded him. Everyone bowed to the mandarin as he passed by. Everyone, that is, except the rich man.

The mandarin noticed the rich man's **impudence** and lowered himself from the sedan to address him. "You there," said the mandarin, pointing to the stonecutter. "Do you know who I am? I am the mandarin. You must bow as everyone else has."

But the rich man refused. "Bow to you? Why should I bow to you? After all, I am a man of enormous wealth!" he boasted.

His pride angered the mandarin. "Guards, arrest that man! Give him a beating that such rudeness deserves. Let it be a lesson that he won't soon forget."

The guards seized the rich man and beat him so badly that he could hardly stand. His servants were called to carry him home.

As the rich man tended to his wounds that evening, he thought about what had happened. "My money was useless against the mandarin's power," he said to himself. "Oh, how I wish I were a mandarin instead of just a rich man!"

The next morning, his servants arrived very early to help him get dressed. But the servants didn't bring his usual rich man's clothing. Strangely, they carried the costume of an official of the first rank.

"What is this?" asked the rich man.

"Why, it is your **attire**, sir. You have several official events today, so we thought you needed an early start."

As he tried to clear his head, the rich man wondered, "Could the gods have granted my wish? Is it true that I really am a mandarin?"

Carefully, he took the costume from his servants. He gently put on the handsome cap decorated with a gold button on the crown. A long, narrow piece of red coral rested on the button. After pausing to admire himself, he

---

[3] A *sedan* is a chair on two long poles carried by four people—two in front and two in back.

put on a violet coat with white cranes sewn on the front and back. Finally he belted the robe with a piece of leather decorated with agates[4] and rubies.

"How impressive I am," he thought to himself. "As a mandarin, I have much more power than a rich man."

So, he spent the next several days **strutting** around the district. He made up new rules and he handed out rewards and punishments according to his mood. The townsfolk quickly learned to fear and hate the transformed stonecutter. This bothered him a bit, but it didn't prevent him from enjoying his new, powerful position.

One morning the new mandarin was strolling through the village when he heard the emperor was drawing near. Common people hurried into buildings and hid behind closed doors. Mandarins and other people of rank dropped to their knees and lowered their heads as the emperor passed. Everyone knew it was forbidden to look at the emperor.

But the mandarin sneaked a forbidden peek at the procession. What he observed was a dazzling sight. First he saw a figure carrying a yellow satin umbrella that glittered in the sunlight. Three rows of fringe gently swayed as the umbrella passed the mandarin. A five-clawed dragon had been carefully embroidered on the top.

Next came the emperor. He was carried in an elegant sedan covered with the same yellow satin. Three rows of fringe hung from his chair. Twelve flags adorned the top.

Escorting the emperor were twenty men on horseback. These were the emperor's sons and brothers. The riders were clothed in jackets of yellow satin, and they carried bows and swords. The procession ended with a hundred or more men on foot, some leading horses.

The mandarin was **awestruck**. "This man is the highest ruler in the land," he said to himself. "One word

---

[4] (ag´ ət) An *agate* is a stone that has various colors arranged in bands.

from him and armies march, laws are made or canceled, and officials are promoted or put to death. Even a high-ranking mandarin like myself is no more to him than a fly that he flicks off his sleeve. Oh, how I wish I were the emperor instead!" Envious and weary, the former stonecutter retired for the night.

The next morning brought another miracle. The stonecutter could hardly believe his eyes when he awoke in the emperor's bedroom. Servants appeared to help him dress. First they helped him step into the imperial robes. They could barely manage the heavy gown, embroidered with the emblems of the sun, moon, and stars. Next they placed the emperor's cap on his head. This was a flat-topped headpiece with jewels hanging from the front and back.

It was true. He was now the emperor.

The new emperor rejoiced in his absolute power. He enjoyed having people bow to him. Never did he tire of hearing people praise his wisdom, even when his actions were foolish or unjust. He knew they did so only out of fear or in hopes of gaining favor. But he didn't care. Affection didn't matter to him as long as he had power.

Then one hot summer day the emperor learned that even his great power had limits. As the blazing sun beat down on the earth, the intense heat made him sweat **profusely**. He was so hot and thirsty that he felt his life was boiling out of him! His royal garments, which were thick and heavy, added to his misery. He ordered four men to create a breeze by waving huge fans, but this gave him no relief.

"What good is being an emperor," he thought to himself, "if I am helpless against the sun's power? Oh, how I wish I were the sun instead of the emperor!"

Once again the gods were listening and heard his wish. As the emperor's servants watched, his body shriveled up in the unbearable heat. But his spirit was transported to the sun. Now he was the Lord of the Heavens.

The new Lord of the Heavens **relished** his fierce power. He used his fiery rays to scorch the land from one end to the other. Streams dried up, and crops withered. All those who toiled beneath the sun cursed him for the heat. But he was enjoying his power too much to care about such puny, unimportant creatures.

One day as he was rolling across the sky radiating his great heat, a strange thing happened. A heavy, dark cloud moved between him and the earth. Annoyed, the sun bellowed, "Move on. You are in my way." But the cloud stayed where it was. So the sun tried to pierce the cloud with his blistering rays. But the cloud didn't budge.

Finally the sun realized that all his efforts couldn't affect the cloud. "My power is **stupendous**," the sun said to himself. "But what's the good of having such power if a cloud can keep me from using it? Oh, how I wish I were a cloud instead of the sun! Then I would be content."

In an instant, the gods transformed him into a huge rain cloud that covered half the sky. Gleefully the cloud let loose a downpour on the earth below. Soon the rivers overflowed their banks, flooding streets and fields, carrying away houses, and drowning people and animals. The people prayed that the cloud would leave. But their prayers fell on deaf ears. The cloud continued to rain on the earth.

Some days later, bursts of rain still fell from the cloud. Suddenly a gust of wind began pushing him.

"Stop shoving!" the cloud snarled at the wind. But the wind kept pushing him until he was over the ocean. There he could do little harm to the land and people.

"It appears that this wind is more powerful than I am," the cloud said to himself. "Oh, how I wish I were the wind instead of a cloud!"

Again the gods granted his wish. The former stonecutter became the wind. He howled with fury as he lashed the countryside with hurricanes and tornadoes, carrying away huts and uprooting trees.

He was having fun blasting the land until he hit

something that he could not budge. It was the side of a mountain. He tried again and again, pushing with all his might, but the mountain didn't move.

"Now I know nothing could be more powerful than this," the wind said. "Oh, how I wish I were a mountain instead of the wind!"

The gods nodded their heads, and there he stood, the tallest, most massive object on earth. He could touch the sky and see as far as the oceans. He **reflected** smugly that no power on earth could move him.

But wait. What was that tapping sound? *Tap, tap. Plink, plink, plink.* He couldn't see where it was coming from, but the sound kept getting louder. *Plink, plink, plink. Chwunk, chwunk.* Then he saw who was making the sound.

It was a stonecutter, pounding chunks of rock out of the mountain's side. Nearby were several **gaping** holes where other pieces had been cut out.

"Alas," the mountain said to himself, "I am immense and immovable, and yet I am slowly being chipped away by a lowly stonecutter. Now I see that there is no power in nature or among men that cannot be overcome. May the gods forgive me for my foolishness! I beg to be a simple stonecutter again."

For the last time, the gods granted his wish. He found himself back in his workshop, putting the finishing touches on his statue of Ts'ai Shen, the God of Wealth. He stood back and surveyed his work with satisfaction. "My skill turned a rough piece of stone into a fine statue," he said to himself. "Why should I wish for any more power than that?"

So, for the rest of his long life, the stonecutter was content.

INSIGHTS

This story probably dates back to the T'ang dynasty in China (618–907 A.D.). The subject of this and many other ancient Chinese myths is power. The Chinese people understand power all too well—from the victim's point of view.

The ancient Chinese had to deal with power from many different sources. One source was the natural environment. The people were at the mercy of nature's forces. When there was a drought, millions died of starvation. When there was too much rain, floods brought famine, disease, and destruction. And entire villages could disappear during an earthquake.

The Chinese were also at the mercy of their rulers. The emperor, who was believed to be the Son of Heaven, had the power of life and death over his subjects. He ruled everyone—from government officials to village clerks. A cruel or corrupt emperor could make life miserable for all people in China.

The emperor, his family, and his trusted ministers and nobles lived in luxury and splendor. The magnificent home of the emperor is called the Forbidden City because common people were not allowed to enter. This vast city still exists in Beijing,[1] although the last emperor's rule in China ended in 1912.

Each year, the emperor led a procession from the Forbidden City to the Temple of Heaven. Because common people were not allowed to see the emperor, they had to hide behind closed doors as he passed by with his court members and soldiers.

The lesson learned by the stonecutter reflects the teachings of two great religions in China, Taoism[2] and

---

[1] (bā´ jing) Beijing, also known as Peking, is the northern capital of China.
[2] (tau´ i zəm)

Buddhism.[3] Taoism emphasizes the importance of living a quiet life in accordance with one's own nature. It teaches that a person should neither strive to rule others nor allow others to rule him or her.

The central teaching of Buddhism is that the desire for power, wealth, and worldly pleasures causes human suffering. Only by giving up these desires can one escape from the endless cycle of birth, death, and rebirth. The stonecutter learns both of these lessons from his experiences in "Wish for Power."

[3] (bü´ di zəm)

THE LUCKY STRAW

VOCABULARY PREVIEW

The following words appear in the story. Review the list and get to know the words before you read the story.

accusation—charge; complaint
adorned—decorated; bedecked
affluent—rich; well-to-do
annoyed—fed up; bothered
begrudged—resented; gave unwillingly
brocade—silk fabric with raised patterns
compassionate—kind; understanding
condescending—snobbish; pompous
consciousness—alertness; awareness
divine—holy; godly
fare—food
graciously—politely
lacquered—coated with a clear, shiny finish
luscious—delicious; juicy
pampered—babied; spoiled
provisions—food and water; supplies for a trip
quench—satisfy; fulfill
scabbard—holder for a sword or blade; sheath
scornfully—critically; doubtfully
scowl—look of displeasure; frown
unblemished—perfect; unmarked
wondrous—awesome; amazing

Main Characters

laborer—poor man
Kannon—goddess of mercy

The poor laborer in this story learns that following a goddess' instructions is well worth the effort.

The Lucky Straw

Adapted from a Japanese tale

There was once a laborer who was very poor. The man was so thin that his ribs and shoulder blades stuck out. His clothes were little better than rags. His poverty did not come from laziness, for he was an honest man and a hard worker. Yet he was never able to make a better life for himself. One day the laborer went to the temple of Hase[1] in Yamoto[2] to pray to Kannon, the Buddhist goddess of mercy. He marveled at the **wondrous** temple made of dark red cherry wood and topped with a huge, sloping, bronze roof. Beautiful carvings of figures **adorned** its walls and columns.

---

[1] (hä´ sa)
[2] (yä mō´ tō) Yamoto is a city in Japan. The city drew its name from the Yamoto clan, who were very powerful people around 400 A.D.

He bowed deeply to the goddess and said, "O **Compassionate** One, please hear my prayer. I have had a hard life. My father died before I was born, and my mother died soon after. I was taken in by a widowed aunt, who had children of her own to feed and **begrudged** me every mouthful. When I was growing up, I thought life would be better for me if I worked hard. But that's not the case. From dawn until darkness I work at whatever I can find. Still my wages barely keep me alive. Please show me a way out of this miserable poverty."

Having finished his prayer, the laborer bowed again and turned to leave. It was still early, and he planned to go about the town seeking work for the day. But suddenly he was overcome with sleepiness. He went to a dim corner of the temple, lay down, and immediately fell asleep.

While he slept, Kannon appeared to the laborer in a dream. She was adorned in fine clothes and surrounded by lotus[3] flowers.

"The reason you are poor," the goddess said, "is that you were selfish and mean in your former life. But you have behaved well in this life, and your prayers are sincere. Therefore, I shall give you a chance to better yourself. Leave the temple and go to Kyoto.[4] The first thing you find in your hand after you leave the temple will help you become wealthy. Take it to Kyoto and use it wisely."

When the man awoke, he remembered the dream but could not understand its meaning. Nevertheless, he decided he had nothing to lose by following the goddess' instructions. He stood up, left the temple, and turned toward the road that led to Kyoto. As he walked through the temple gates, he tripped and fell. His head hit a rock, and he lost **consciousness**.

When the laborer came out of the daze, he found a piece of straw in his hand. "How did I get this? There is

---

[3] A *lotus* is a water lily that symbolizes the flowering of the human spirit.
[4] (kē ō′ tō) Kyoto was the capital city of Japan from 784 to 1868.

no straw around here, just dust from the road. Perhaps this is a sign from Kannon," he thought.

It seemed unlikely to the poor laborer that a piece of straw could lead to a better life. But he held on to it nevertheless. "Better to keep it than risk offending the goddess by tossing it aside," he thought. So he dusted himself off and continued on the journey to Kyoto.

He had not gone far when a horsefly began bothering him. It buzzed around his head, biting his ear and the back of his neck. As often as he brushed the fly away, it came back to pester him. Finally he caught the fly in his hands. He was about to crush it, but he could not. The thought came to him that it too wanted to live. So instead of killing it, he tied it to the end of the straw.

He was walking along with the horsefly buzzing cheerfully on the end of the straw when he met an ox-drawn cart. Inside was a well-to-do woman, her children, and their servants. Suddenly the cart stopped, and the mother and her little boy stepped down.

"My youngest son saw you walking with your horsefly," the woman said as they approached. "He thinks it's the most charming toy he has ever seen. Would you be so kind as to give it to him?"

The laborer glanced at the little boy. He was obviously a **pampered** child, who was used to getting whatever he wanted. The laborer remembered his own childhood and how he had been put to work in the rice paddies almost as soon as he could walk. He had never even had enough food, much less toys. Still, he understood how a child felt when he had set his heart on something.

"Dear lady," he said, "this is a gift from the goddess Kannon. But if the young one really wants it, then he shall have it."

"Thank you," she said as she handed him a package wrapped in white paper. "Here, please accept this small gift in return for your kindness."

When the carriage had driven off, the laborer opened

the package. Inside were three **luscious** oranges! They were round, firm, and **unblemished**. Their tangy fragrance made the laborer's mouth water. But he did not think of eating them. He knew the goddess meant him to sell them for a good price in Kyoto. Besides, he thought, the stomach of a laborer is not used to such delicate **fare**.

Still as he continued on his way, he couldn't resist unwrapping the oranges occasionally to enjoy their fragrance. Once as he held the orange to his nose, he felt someone watching him. The laborer looked around and saw a woman and two young men resting under a nearby tree. The three looked like wilted flowers.

The woman signaled him to come closer. "Please, sir," she said, "can you tell us where we might get a drink? My brothers and I are dying of thirst, and we have such a long way to go." As she spoke, she looked longingly at the oranges.

The laborer was **annoyed**. These three obviously belonged to an **affluent** family. They should have brought along servants and **provisions**. Instead, here they were, asking help from a poor stranger who could ill afford to give it. But when he saw how weak and close to death they looked, he felt sorry for them.

"No, there's no place around here where you can get a drink," he answered. "But if you like, I will give you these oranges. They might **quench** your thirst."

The thirsty travellers eagerly accepted the oranges. All smiled with delight while putting a juicy section into their mouths.

"You have saved our lives," said the woman as she ate the fruit. "Had you not come along, who knows what would have happened? I must insist that you take these three rolls of cloth. They are all we have with us."

Graciously the man took the rolls of cloth and went on his way. He had walked only a short distance when he stumbled and dropped the load he was carrying. As the rolls of cloth fell, they unwound, and the laborer saw the rich fabrics. One roll was heavy red silk, one was green silk with a design of silver leaves, and one was a **brocade** of many colors. He wondered if this could be Kannon's latest gift.

Just then a fierce-looking samurai[6] paraded by, leading a band of soldiers. He was riding a tall horse covered with a red decorative blanket. He wore leather armor and carried two swords in **scabbards** of **lacquered** wood. He looked around him with a **scowl**, which softened somewhat when his glance fell on the cloth.

He stopped his horse and spoke to the laborer in a **condescending** tone. "That's not bad cloth, although I've seen much better. I need something to give to my wife when I get home. I believe this will do."

"But, sir," the laborer protested, "this is a gift from the goddess Kannon."

"Why would a goddess give you a gift?" asked the samurai **scornfully**. "I think it's much more likely that you stole it. If so, confess it now, and I won't whip you."

The laborer couldn't help feeling angry at the samurai's false **accusation** of stealing. But his anger was mixed with pity. "His actions will catch up with him," thought the poor laborer. "Buddha says each person's position in the next life is determined by behavior in the previous life. Because of his bad temper, this samurai has already stored up suffering for himself in his next life." Then he thought, "If I let him go on with these false accusations, he'll be even worse off."

The laborer gathered up the rolls of cloth and offered them to the samurai with a bow. "If I lose Kannon's gift through no fault of my own, she will give me another," he said. "Here is the cloth, sir. You are welcome to it."

These words seemed to embarrass the samurai. He answered quickly, "What? Did you think I would take your cloth and not give you anything in return? Such meanness would be far beneath me! No, I want you to take that gray horse that my servant is leading. It is one of my best."

---

[6] (sa´ mə rī) The samurai were respected warriors who protected *shoguns*. Shoguns were lords who controlled huge estates.

The laborer thanked the samurai for his generosity. Then he climbed onto his new horse and continued down the road to Kyoto. He could hardly believe his good luck. "First I was given a straw, then some oranges, then some cloth, and now this splendid horse. Truly, that straw was a **divine** gift."

A short while later, the laborer arrived in Kyoto atop his fine horse. He passed a large house. At the front gate, servants were loading household goods into carriages.

"That's a fine horse you have there," said the owner of the house. "I really need a riding horse, but I'm short of cash just now." He stopped speaking and seemed to be deep in thought. After a moment he continued. "I know you'd hate to part with such a valuable animal. But I have a small rice field I'll be leaving behind after I move. How would you like to have it in exchange for your horse?"

"I would like that very much," the laborer said.

"Then it's a bargain!" said the man. "And if you like, you may live in my house until I return."

From a piece of straw to a field in one day! The laborer was so overwhelmed that he could scarcely find words to thank the man.

Time passed, and soon the laborer was no longer poor. With the profits from the small rice field, he bought other pieces of land. He married the daughter of a well-to-do family in the region and had several children. For unknown reasons, the former owner of the farm never returned. So in time, the man also got the house and rice fields. Eventually he became one of the richest landholders in the district.

But no matter how great his fortune grew, the man never forgot that it had started with the gift of a straw. And every year on the anniversary of that gift, he went to the temple in Yamoto to give thanks to Kannon.

INSIGHTS

"The Lucky Straw" is a legend from Japan. Japan is a nation made up of four large islands and many small islands off the eastern edge of the Asian continent. Because most of the country is mountainous, only about sixteen percent of the land is suitable for growing crops. "The Lucky Straw" takes place when most of the land was controlled by a few rich and powerful families. Thus, to acquire even a small rice field would be a tremendous stroke of luck for a poor laborer.

The samurai who exchanges one of his finest horses for cloth was a member of a class of warriors. Just as nobility handed down titles from parent to child, samurai handed their titles down to their sons. Samurai were trained to fight on horseback with sword and bow and arrow. They follow a strict code of behavior that called for absolute obedience and loyalty to the nobles they served. They were proud of their strength and their ability to endure pain without flinching. Many stories tell of samurai who commit suicide rather than disgrace their lord and themselves by surrendering to an enemy.

In "The Lucky Straw" when the samurai comes along, the laborer comments on the samurai's spirit. Buddhists believe that a person's existence is a continuous cycle of life and death. The actions and deeds of each person determine his or her position in the next life.

For example, good deeds may lead to rebirth as a wise and wealthy person. Evil deeds may lead to rebirth as a poor or sick person. The only way to break out of this cycle is to gain a perfect peace and happiness that Buddha calls *Nirvana.*[1] To do this, a person must give up all attachments to worldly things and follow a strict life.

[1] (nir vä´ nə)

Kannon, the goddess of mercy mentioned in this tale, is one of the most beloved deities in Japanese Buddhism. She is a *bodhisattva.*[2] A bodhisattva is a person who, like the Buddha, has attained enlightenment. However, unlike Buddha, bodhisattvas do not enter Nirvana. Instead they remain on earth to help others find the path to enlightenment.

---

[2] (bōh di sat´ wa)

A · S · I · A · n

LOVE

Bride's Island

The Ruby Ring

Two Brothers

Compassion. Devotion. Admiration. These three qualities form the core of human love in Asian myths.

A high value is placed on family bonds in Asian cultures. Many myths are about people who test this relationship. But even though these bonds may be tested, they are never broken.

Asian stories also feature romantic love. They tell of lovers who overcome impossible obstacles to show their devotion. Often someone makes a great sacrifice for the benefit of a loved one.

You'll see the strength of human love in the next three stories.

M · y · T · h · S

BRIDE'S ISLAND

VOCABULARY PREVIEW

The following words appear in the story. Review the list and get to know the words before you read the story.

ailing—sick; ill
comprehend—understand; take in
engulfed—submerged; overwhelmed
gravely—seriously; dangerously
heed—obey; follow; listen to
hideous—beastly; frightful
perilous—dangerous
predicted—foresaw; foretold
remedy—cure; treatment
resumed—started again; began again
tapered—pointed; more narrow at one end than the other
transformed—changed; altered
undulating—rising and falling
writhing—twisting; coiling

Main Characters

fisherman—dying groom
fisherman's wife—brave, devoted bride
shaman—priestess

Bride's Island

A beautiful bride never returns from a secretive trip. Soon after, a hideous serpent visits her cottage. Her new husband is so overcome by grief that he also disappears. Are the two lovers ever rejoined? Read their story and see what you think.

Adapted from a Korean tale

A joyful wedding took place one day in a small fishing village by the sea. The groom was a young fisherman, and the bride was the loveliest girl in the village. Everyone **predicted** that the couple would have a long, happy marriage. It was clear they loved each other deeply.

But their happiness wasn't meant to last. Ten days after the wedding the husband became **gravely** ill. His wife tried every **remedy** she could think of, but he grew steadily worse. Night and day she prayed to the Mountain God for an end to his illness. But no help came.

One morning an old shaman[1] happened by while the bride was praying. This shaman had many powers. She could see into the future. She could also speak with the gods and the spirits of dead ancestors. As the shaman passed, she saw the devoted bride praying beside her husband. She stopped to listen.

After praying for so many days, the bride had grown frustrated. "Once again I pray to you, and you send me no answers. Why do you choose to ignore me?"

"Do not speak angry words," said the shaman from the door.

The bride was surprised to hear a voice behind her.

"The gods cannot help you," the shaman continued. "The remedy is not that simple."

"Are you saying there is no way to save him?" asked the young woman.

"There is always a way," responded the shaman.

"If you know of a remedy, you must tell me," said the young wife, rising to her feet. "I'd go to the ends of the earth to find it."

The shaman hesitated. Then she said, "I can recall one plant that could cure him. But it's so difficult to find that no one I know has ever seen it."

"Where is it? What do I have to do to get it?" asked the wife eagerly.

"It's in a place so **perilous** that even I'm afraid to go there."

"Well, I'm not!" declared the young woman.

The shaman replied, "A few others have said those words and have gone in search of the plant. Not one of them ever returned."

"I am willing to risk my life to help my husband," said the wife. "If he dies, I will die of grief anyway. So please, I beg of you, give me a chance to save him."

Realizing how determined the young wife was, the shaman took her seriously. She sat down beside the wife and took the young woman's hands in her own.

[1] (shä´ mən) A *shaman* is a priest or priestess who uses magic to cure the sick.

"The magical plant can only be found in one place. It grows on the smallest island in the Seven Mountains group. You can see the island from here. It is known as Serpent's Island, and it is said that an evil god rules the island. Please **heed** my warning. I beg you not to go."

"I have no choice. I must go."

"Then may the gods be with you."

The next day the young woman prepared for the trip. She told her husband that she was going to get a medicinal plant that would help him. Not wanting to worry him, she didn't mention her destination. She took her husband's fishing boat and set off for the island.

The island wasn't far from shore, so she arrived in a short time. Looking around, she wondered how to begin her search. Suddenly she realized, "I don't even know what this mysterious plant looks like." Then she reassured herself, "Surely, if it's magical, it will look different from the other plants." She began walking slowly through the brush, scanning the ground as she went.

The young woman searched for several hours without finding anything unusual. She was beginning to feel discouraged when she noticed a pine tree that stood apart from the others. Around the foot of the tree was a bed of thick green grass. She walked over to the grass and bent down to examine it. Each shining blade was curved and **tapered** like a serpent's fang.

"This must be the magic plant!" she thought. Setting down her bamboo basket, she began to fill it with large handfuls of the grass. Its sharp points scratched her hands and wrists. But in her excitement she hardly felt the pain. She was sure she had found what she was looking for. Her husband would live!

Unexpectedly, a noise like a long sigh came from the grass. "Is someone there?" she asked. When there was no answer, she **resumed** picking the grass.

The sigh came again, but this time it sounded more like a hiss. Then the ground began to rise and fall in a rippling motion. The hissing sound grew louder and louder. As she watched in horror, one of the ripples rose up and became a large snake. The serpent was brown, with a row of diamond-shaped black spots along each side. A black spot on the top of its head sparkled like a crown. The snake opened its mouth, flicked its forked tongue, and hissed. Green venom dripped from long, curved fangs.

The young woman screamed and tried to stand, determined to grab the basket and run back to the boat. But now hundreds of **writhing** snakes were all around her. She was **engulfed** in a sea of scales and hisses. Some wrapped their **undulating** coils around her, while others rose to strike. She screamed again and closed her eyes as the **hideous** creatures hurled themselves at her. Then everything went black.

When she came to her senses, she was lying full length on her stomach. The ground was solid and unmoving. Nearby she could see her bamboo basket filled with grass.

"The snakes did not kill me after all," she thought joyfully. "I can still save my husband."

She had a vision of her husband drinking tea made from the magic plant and immediately sitting up in bed and laughing. She tried to close her eyes in order to see this happy vision more clearly. But, to her amazement, her eyelids refused to move.

As she tried to get up, her legs seemed to be wrapped tightly together. Her arms, too, seemed to be fastened to her sides. Now she was frightened. She opened her mouth to cry to the Mountain God for help. But what came out were not words—it was a hiss! Turning her head, she looked down at her body. Instead of seeing the form of a young woman, she saw a long, scaly body. She had been **transformed** into a serpent!

For a few minutes she lay silent, unable to **comprehend** this horrible situation. Then she thought, "Although I have changed outside, the love I feel inside for my husband will never change. I have come this far for his sake. I must not give up." She picked up as much of the magic grass as she could hold in her mouth and slithered to the shore. She swam across the narrow stretch of water that separated her village from the island. Then she crawled into the village.

The villagers couldn't believe their eyes. A huge brown serpent with its mouth full of grass was slithering through the village. Everyone stood aside and let the creature pass.

One woman whispered to her young son, "Run and fetch the old shaman. Hurry!"

The boy dashed to the house of the shaman, who was tending to her garden. "Come quickly," he cried. "A big snake came out of the water, and it has grass in its mouth!"

The villagers followed the snake at a safe distance to see where it would go. By the time the boy and the shaman arrived, the snake had reached the cottage of the **ailing** fisherman. It slithered inside the house and put its mouthful of grass on a table. Then it turned and moved out of the house. As it came to the door, it looked up and saw the shaman standing close by. The two made eye contact and seemed to understand each other.

The serpent began to move quickly back to the shore. As it reached the water's edge, the serpent turned and looked back at the village. Then it slipped into the water and swam toward Serpent's Island.

What happened next is still a mystery. As the villagers watched the snake swim away, some say that Serpent's Island took on a new shape. The closer the snake got to the island, the more the outline of the shore looked like a young woman. In fact, some villagers claimed the island changed to the shape of the bride.

As the villagers watched this strange transformation, the shaman hurried back to the fisherman's house. She made a strong tea from the grass brought by the snake. Then she gently helped the young groom drink the hot brew.

The fisherman began to get better right away. In a few days, he was completely cured of the strange ailment. And he started to ask about his missing wife.

In time the shaman told the fisherman what his young wife had done. The fisherman went wild with grief. Before anyone could stop him, he ran to the shore and jumped into a fishing boat. Then he furiously paddled to the island. He disappeared into the mist and was never heard from again.

The villagers began calling the island Bride's Island in honor of the wife's sacrifice for her husband. And that's what it's called to this day.

It's generally believed that the Mountain God took pity on the unfortunate couple and reunited them. Some say he did this by turning the husband into a snake. Others say the god restored the wife to her human form. Of course, nobody knows for sure.

INSIGHTS

The Korean people descended from tribes that originally lived in Manchuria[1] and Siberia.[2] The native religion of these first tribes was shamanism. Sometime before 2000 B.C., these tribes migrated south and settled in the Korean peninsula.

As people from other countries migrated to this area, religious beliefs diversified. China brought Buddhism, and Japan introduced Confucianism to Korea. Eventually, Western missionaries introduced Christianity. Confucianism, Buddhism, and Christianity had a powerful influence on Korean life and culture, but they never replaced shamanism.

The shaman in this story would likely have been a woman. Before the influence of China and Japan, women in the Korean culture held important roles in society. Among the Koreans' tribal ancestors, the shaman was a combination of a religious leader, healer, and wizard.

A shaman's power was based on the ability to go into a trance. While in a trance, the shaman's spirit could leave his or her body and travel anywhere in the cosmos. The shaman could also communicate with supernatural beings. These supernatural beings included demons, spirits of dead ancestors, and spirits of natural objects, such as mountains, streams, and trees. The shaman could call on these beings for help in healing the sick and interpreting dreams.

Today, almost all Korean shamans are women. One of their important functions is to perform rituals in honor of a family's ancestors and household gods. During the celebration, the shaman may dance and sing herself into a

[1] (man chür´ ē ə) Manchuria is a region in Northeast China. It is bordered by North Korea, Mongolia, and the former Soviet Union.
[2] (si bir´ ē ə) Siberia is the most northern territory of Asia. Its borders touch the Arctic Ocean and include the cold region of the tundra.

trance. She may then allow gods and spirits to use her voice to scold or give advice to various members of the audience.

Korea's rich tradition of folk literature includes fairy tales, novellas, hero tales, sagas, myths, fables, legends, and jests. The oldest surviving examples of Korean folktales are contained in the *Samguk yusa,*[3] which dates back to the late 13th century.

This collection includes some unusual stories based on traditions of Buddhism and shamanism. The shaman stories often involve adventures in which the main character searches for a life-giving herb, very much like the young wife in "Bride's Island."

---

[3] (säm´ gŭk ūsă) Samguk yusa translates to "Remnants of the Three Kingdoms."

THE RUBY RING

VOCABULARY PREVIEW

The following words appear in the story. Review the list and get to know the words before you read the story.

alit—gently landed; descended
basin—sink; container
boughs—branches; limbs
court—try to win the affection of; date
destiny—future; fate
dismissed—sent away
flitting—moving quickly from one point to the next; darting
idleness—leisure; ease; goofing off
lenient—easygoing; kind
luxuries—comforts; fine things
migration—movement; journey
pursuit—chase; hunt; mission
splendor—richness; beauty; elegance
sternly—firmly; strictly
suitors—men looking for a wife; admirers; boyfriends
sullen—sad; moody
supernatural—unusual; superhuman; fantastic
symmetrical—well-proportioned; balanced

Main Characters

Linh—princess
Nak—prince; suitor of Linh
the king—Linh's father
maid—Princess Linh's servant

A charming princess hopes for a husband. But her father sets impossible tests for her suitors. Can she find a truly noble man who can prove his love for her by doing what can't be done?

The Ruby Ring

Adapted from a Cambodian myth

Once there was a young princess named Linh[1] whose father was the most powerful king in all the lands. She lived in her father's palace on the banks of the Mekong[2] River. Royal **suitors** from neighboring lands came to ask the king for his daughter's hand in marriage. Of course, these suitors might have been drawn by something else besides the promise of a kingdom. Linh was also very beautiful.

But each suitor received a cold welcome from the king. When a young man asked permission to marry the princess, the king **sternly** said, "You must prove that you are worthy of my clever daughter. Only the strongest, bravest, and smartest man in the land shall marry her. To prove you are worthy, you must complete several difficult tasks."

[1] (lin)
[2] (mā´ kon)

The king spent all his spare moments thinking up impossible tasks. Since the suitors were sensible men, all gave up and returned home when they heard the requirements. Each would say, "No one can do what can't be done."

Princess Linh began to worry as she saw suitor after suitor turned away. Finally after the eighth one had been **dismissed**, she asked her father to be more **lenient**.

"I fear you are putting too high a value on me, Father," she said. "You are making the suitors' tests too difficult. Perhaps no one will ever succeed, and I will never marry."

"Better not to marry at all than to marry an inferior man," declared the king.

"But, Father, these tests don't measure real character or ability. These tests are impossible! Only a **supernatural** being could pass them."

"No, Daughter. A truly superior human *can* do the impossible. Such a man may still come along. Have faith, Daughter, and trust my judgment."

Linh knew it was useless to argue with her father. All she could do was bow to him and quietly walk away. The months passed, and suitor after suitor gave up the quest to marry Linh. The princess grew **sullen** and quiet, keeping company with no one.

One day her maid returned from an errand with exciting news. "As I was getting your bathwater from the well, a kind and noble young traveler came along."

"How could you tell? What was he like?" asked the princess eagerly.

"He was tall and strong," replied the maid. "He had clear, very dark eyes. There was a peaceful expression on his face, and he spoke in a kind tone. His words sounded like sweet music. I think he may be in our village still."

"What did he say?" asked Linh.

"He asked for a drink of water. So I invited him to drink from the vessel of water I had just drawn. He dipped his hands into the water, held them to his lips, and drank. Then he thanked me politely and sat down to rest. I hurried home to tell you."

Linh's heart began to beat faster as she listened to the maid's story. Could this be the man who could pass the king's impossible tests? "Go find him at once," she ordered. "If he is still here, find out where he is going."

The maid rushed out. Linh gazed into the **basin** from which the charming young man had drunk. As she looked, she noticed a soft glow at the bottom of the basin. She plunged her hand in and lifted out a heavy gold ring set with a large ruby. It was the kind of ring that only a prince would wear.

Linh was thrilled at the sight of this ring. She could tell it was a sign that the owner of this ring would be her prince.

When Linh's maid reached the village, she found the young man at the well. He was pacing back and forth, his eyes fixed on the ground. "I have lost my ring," he said. "It was a gift from my father, and I can't leave here until I find it."

"What does it look like? I will help you search," said the maid.

"It is a gold ring with one ruby."

As they searched, the maid said to the young man, "My mistress desires to know where you are going."

"I'm going nowhere in particular," said the young man. "That is, I will eventually arrive at some place in particular, but right now I don't know where that place will be." He bent to examine an object on the ground. He kicked it aside when he realized it was not his ring.

The maid waited a moment to see whether he would go on talking. When he did not, she said, "If I give that answer to my mistress, she will only send me back to question you further."

The young man stopped searching for a moment, put aside his frustrations, and said, "Then I'll try to explain. You see, my father is the king of a land far to the south. Of his many sons, I am the youngest and least important. I could have stayed home and lived a life of **idleness**. But with the **luxuries** of a prince, I would have been of no use to myself or others. So instead, I decided to go out into the world and see what else fate has to offer me."

"How did you know which way to go?"

"Oh, I didn't. I simply followed the signs that **destiny** put in my way. If I saw a tree uprooted by a storm, I went where it pointed. Or if I heard a bird singing in the distance or saw the sun shine brightly on a certain hill, I went in that direction. Sometimes the signs led me to a place where I found food and shelter. Sometimes they led me to a place where a person or animal needed my help.

"Along the way I saw many wonderful sights. To the west I found mountains covered with forests of cardamom trees. Turning north, I came to a huge lake so crowded with fish that the people could hardly row their boats through the water. Near that lake was a river that flows backwards during part of the year."

"And so at last the signs led you here," the maid interrupted.

"Yes, and I think that losing my ring may be a sign that I should stay for a while."

The maid knew the princess would be wondering where she was. "I will go now and report to my mistress," said the maid.

"By the way, who is your mistress?" asked the young man.

"She is Princess Linh, the daughter of the king of this land."

"I am Prince Nak.[3] Please give my respectful greetings to the princess."

The maid hurried back to Linh and told her all that she had learned.

"Go back once more," ordered the princess. "Tell Prince Nak that his ring will be returned to him by my own hand."

Once more, the maid went to Prince Nak with news of his ring. When Nak heard this, he knew that fate had guided him to his destiny. "Please show me the way to the palace," he said to the maid. "I must see this resourceful princess."

[3] (nak)

As the maid and the prince walked back to the palace, she told him of the difficult tasks that faced the princess' suitors. She spoke of the princess' talents and why all the suitors had failed to win her hand. Finally the two arrived at the palace, and Nak was led into the throne room. There he saw the king seated on a high platform and the princess seated beside him on a slightly lower platform. Nak and Linh took one look at each other and fell deeply in love.

The king, ignoring the shy glances and smiles that were **flitting** back and forth between the two, greeted Nak with his usual coldness. Nak knelt before the king and asked permission to **court** the princess. He gave Nak the same answer he had given all the other suitors, "My daughter is precious to me. You must prove that you are worthy of her."

"How may I do that, your majesty?" asked Nak.

"You must perform a task to prove your abilities. If you succeed, you may continue your **pursuit**. If you fail, you will never marry my daughter."

"Tell me the task, your majesty."

"You must go to the four corners of the kingdom and bring back the tallest branch from each tree. However, all this must be done before the sun sets."

The prince's heart sank, for it would not be possible to travel such distance and climb to such heights in the few hours of remaining daylight. "Nevertheless, to show my love for the princess, I will try," thought the prince.

After the king's servants finished tying ribbons to the highest **boughs** in all the kingdom, Nak set out to the east. He had not been walking long when a bird **alit** on his shoulder.

"Do you remember me?" the bird asked. "A while ago you saved me from a clouded leopard[4] who was about to eat me. Now it's my turn to help you." Having said this, the bird called all her friends.

"Hello, my feathered pretties. Today we have an important job. We must work together to help a friend of the flyers," said the bird.

[4] A clouded leopard is a large cat with a grayish-brown coat. It is marked with dark, black-edged patches. It preys mostly on birds and small mammals.

"What is the task?" asked a pink-necked fruit dove.

"The king has placed a bow on the tallest branch in each corner of the kingdom. I suggest we break into four groups and return with the branches."

"How will we pluck a branch with our small beaks?" asked the gold-fronted leafbird.

"This is a problem," said the bird thoughtfully. "I know, break it off with your weight. Stand on it and jump up and down. When it breaks off, simply spread your wings and let the air catch you."

"How will we carry it?" asked the sandpiper.

"In your **migration**, surely you have found gentle currents that will help your group coast back. If everyone takes a leaf from the branch in his or her mouth, you can carefully fly it back."

With that, the birds set out to the four corners of the kingdom. Just before sunset, each group returned with a branch. "Thank you, my friends," Nak said to the birds as four limbs were dropped at his feet. Nak carried the precious branches back to the king.

"You did it!" the king exclaimed when Nak gave him the branches tied with ribbons. But just to make sure, he had his prime minister check each tree.

Then the king said, "I see I shall have to test you again with something harder."

"Another test, your highness? I thought there would be only one, and then I would have Linh's hand."

"No, you misunderstood. I said that you could continue your pursuit. Maybe you don't think she is worth another test of your ability."

"She is worth a thousand tests," said Nak.

"Well then, tomorrow my servants will take a bag of a thousand tiny white pebbles and scatter them in the river. Your task will be to get them all back in the bag by nightfall."

"This seems to be an impossible task," said Nak. "Nevertheless, to show my love for the princess, I will try."

The next morning Nak sat on the riverbank and watched the king's servants scatter the pebbles. But this time he didn't set to work as soon as they left. This time he feared the task was truly hopeless.

As he sat there almost weeping, a fish swam close to the bank and spoke to him. "Hello, my friend. Why the sad face?"

Nak explained his love for the princess and the task he was to complete.

When Nak had finished his story, the fish spoke, "You may not remember me, but you once set me free from a fisherman's trap. Now it's my turn to help you."

The fish then called on all the other fish in that part of the river to help collect the pebbles. As they worked, the fish brought the pebbles to Nak one by one and dropped them into the prince's hand.

At last all the pebbles were back in the bag except one. That pebble had been picked up by the trey ktchoung,[5] who now refused to give it to Nak.

The other fish were shocked. "Why would you want to spoil things for Nak?" they asked. "Don't you want him to marry the princess and be happy?"

"Not particularly," said the trey ktchoung. "Why should I go out of my way to make somebody else happy?"

Hearing the argument, Nak called out, "Who is this powerful fish who holds my fate in his mouth? Please swim over here. I would like to see you."

"I'll bet you would. Then you could grab me," called the trey.

"You must be the most clever fish in this whole river. How fast can you swim?"

"Very fast," said the trey, as he sped around the shallow area.

"Impressive. But can you jump into the air?" asked Nak.

"Naturally," said the trey, jumping in and out of the water.

"That's incredible. What a beautiful snout you have."

[5] (trā k chün´) The trey ktchoung is a spiny eel.

"Everyone is *very* jealous of it," the trey said, tilting back his head.

"Do you have any bright coloring?" asked Nak.

"You're looking at me. See my red fin?" asked the trey, as he turned onto his side.

"Are you sure that's red? From here it seems to be a brownish color."

"No. It is red," said the trey, as he swam a bit closer to the shore.

"Is one fin smaller than the other?" asked Nak. "That's the way it looks from here."

"Of course not. They are perfectly **symmetrical**." With that comment, the trey swam right next to the edge, and Nak reached in and grabbed him.

"Give me that pebble," ordered Nak. But the fish kept his jaws tightly closed and refused to give it up. So Nak pulled and pulled on the fish's snout.

"Ouch!" said the trey, dropping the pebble. "My nose! My beautiful nose! You stretched it and bent it out of shape."

"I am very sorry, trey. Please forgive me. However, I need this pebble to complete my task," said Nak. With a thousand pebbles in the bag, he went to see the king.

"Very impressive!" said the king when all of the tiny pebbles were accounted for. "But you must still pass one more test. Come back tomorrow morning."

The next morning the king led Nak into a room that overlooked the palace garden. In one corner of the room, he saw a tightly woven bamboo screen. Sticking out of nine holes in the screen were nine hands.

"This will be your final and most difficult task. My daughter designed it herself. You must pick the hand of the princess. Which one is it?" the king asked Nak.

Nak took one look and gave a joyful laugh. Of course, it was the hand that wore his own ruby ring! The princess had planned it well.

Soon after that, the wedding of the prince and princess was celebrated with all the **splendor** her father could afford. And, as far as anybody knows, they lived happily ever after.

INSIGHTS

Nak had to go through a series of tests to show Princess Linh's father that he was a fit husband for her. Many Cambodians still observe a similar custom. Prospective bridegrooms often have to gain their in-laws' approval by living with them for a time before the marriage.

There are several references to places in this story. The Cardamom Mountains are located in southwestern Cambodia. They are named for the tall, treelike plants that grow there. The seeds of these plants are used as a spice in cooking.

The huge lake that Nak saw is the Tonle Sap[1] (Great Lake), the largest freshwater lake in Southeast Asia. During the dry season, it's twenty-two miles wide and covers about one thousand square miles. During the rainy season, it grows to four times that size.

The Great Lake is linked to the Mekong River by a channel called the Tonle Sap River. This river really does flow backwards for part of the year, as Nak said. During the dry season (November to May), water flows east from the lake and feeds into the Mekong River. During the rainy season (June to October), the river rises and sends water back into the lake, which then floods the surrounding plains.

The *trey ktchoung* is one of several species of spiny eel that live in the lakes and rivers of Southeast Asia. It is not as snake-like as a true eel. However, it is rather long and narrow, and it has a very flexible body. It also has sharp spines along the middle of its back and on the sides of its head. Nak would probably have cut his skin when he grabbed the fish's snout.

Depending on its age, the *trey ktchoung* can be anywhere from thumb-length to almost three feet long.

[1] (tän lä´ sap)

When the water is low, it's easy to catch several small or medium-size *trey ktchoung* at one time. Just scrape a pail along the bottom near the edge of the lake or river and pour the contents out on dry land. This will give you, in one great swoop, the makings of a bountiful dinner.

TWO BROTHERS

VOCABULARY PREVIEW

The following words appear in the story. Review the list and get to know the words before you read the story.

confirmed—proven; supported
conspiracy—plan; plot
disheveled—unkempt; wild
distress—agony; torment
exhume—dig up; unbury
inherit—obtain or receive after the death of a relative
obedient—dutiful; meek
regarded—considered; thought of
retrieved—returned; brought back
wailed—cried; shrieked

Main Characters

Hai—older brother
Ba—younger brother
Hai's wife—tricks the two brothers

Two Brothers

Murder. Shame. Unfaithful friends. All these threaten to destroy Hai's comfortable status. As he tries to avoid disgrace, he learns what is really important in life.

Adapted from a Vietnamese myth

There was once a man who had a wife and two sons. The elder son was named Hai[1] and the younger Ba.[2]

Although the parents loved both sons equally, they smiled more when they looked at Ba. Perhaps it was because Ba had a pleasant, easygoing manner that lightened their mood and seemed to make their work easier. When something went wrong, he could usually make them see the humor in it. And he was always ready to entertain them with a story told in his own special way. Instead of just describing what happened, he would act it out, using a different voice for each character.

---

[1] (hī)
[2] (bä)

Everyone who knew Ba responded to his charm. The house was often filled with friends and neighbors who dropped in just to listen to Ba talk. As for Hai, he sat against the wall, unnoticed. Hai wasn't as carefree and pleasing as his younger brother. He was more serious and quiet.

In fact, you might say he was jealous of the attention given to his brother. But he had a plan to get even. "Never mind," Hai often said to himself. "Let him have the attention now. I have one thing that Ba doesn't have—the rights of the firstborn. When our parents die, I'll **inherit** everything. Then we shall see how far his charm gets him!"

In due time, their parents got old and died. Hai took possession of all the family's property. He gave Ba a tiny hut and a small plot of poor land in a corner of the property. He kept the rest for himself.

As the years passed, Hai prospered. He lived very comfortably, and he was proud of all that he owned. Every time he entered his house, he noted with satisfaction that several objects in it were worth a lot of money. One of these was a carved jade green bowl from China.

Ba, on the other hand, lived in poverty. Even though he worked hard, his land was so poor that he barely made enough to live on. His elder brother knew of his **distress** but never did anything to help him.

Toward his friends, however, Hai's behavior was just the opposite. Any friend who dropped by at dinnertime got a good meal. If that same friend asked for a loan, he got that too. Hai became known for his generosity and seemed to have a great many friends. He **regarded** himself a popular fellow.

Hai's wife was a sensible young woman who didn't approve of his neglect of Ba. She would ask Hai, "Why do you give so much to your friends but so little to your brother? Your charity should begin with Ba."

"I don't want to spoil him," Hai said. "If I took care of all his needs, he would come to depend on me. It's better to let him stand on his own two feet."

"But you don't mind letting your friends depend on you."

"My friends are devoted to me. They deserve every favor they get." Hai waved his hand at his wife, which meant the discussion was over.

A few times Hai's wife suggested that Ba be invited to dinner along with Hai's friends. But Hai would just glare and ask distrustfully, "Why are you so eager to have him near? Has he captured your heart?" So after a while, she let the matter drop.

Ba accepted the place of an **obedient** younger brother without complaint. He was aware of his sister-in-law's opinions but never discussed the subject with her or with anyone else.

One afternoon Hai came home to find his wife pacing the floor and wringing her hands in great distress. Her hair was **disheveled**, and she had obviously been weeping. "Husband!" she cried. "Something terrible has happened that I fear will bring death to me and disgrace to you."

"What is it?" asked Hai, alarmed. "Tell me quickly!"

"A beggar came to the door asking for food. I told him to wait a few minutes and went to get him a bowl of rice. But when I was gone, the beggar sneaked into the house. As I came out of the kitchen, I saw him grab our carved jade bowl and dash out the door. I ran after him and threw the rice bowl at him. The bowl missed, but the sight of it flying past his ear must have startled him. He stumbled and fell to one knee. This gave me a chance to . . . to . . ." Here she broke off and burst into tears.

"Calm yourself," pleaded Hai. "Go on. What happened then?"

His wife took a deep breath and continued. "While I ran to get a bamboo stick, he slowly rose to his feet and tried to run again. I was worried he'd get away, so I pursued him and swung the bamboo stick with all my strength. This time I got him, and he stumbled, falling forward on his face. I got ready to hit him again, but he didn't get up. He didn't move at all. Then I saw that his head had struck a rock, and he was dead. Oh, Hai, what will become of me now?"

Hai looked at her with a worried frown. Then he brightened. "It seems to me that it wasn't your fault," he said. "It was an accident."

"Falling on the rock was an accident. But he fell because I hit him."

"Perhaps, but you were protecting our property. You hit him because he was a thief."

"Yes, that's true," said the wife. "I **retrieved** the jade bowl and put it back on the shelf where it belongs."

"You fool!" shouted Hai angrily. "You should have left it by the body and called someone to be a witness. That person could have **confirmed** your story. Now you have no proof that he stole the jade bowl and hit his head accidentally!"

The wife hid her face in her hands. "You are right," she **wailed**. "I behaved stupidly. But I was so frightened I couldn't think straight."

"Where is the body?" Hai asked.

"There," said his wife, pointing. "I rolled it up in that mat and dragged it in here where no one would see it."

Hai thought for a moment. Then he said, "What we must do is bury the body and act as if nothing has happened."

"Yes," said the wife. "Let us do it tonight. We'll have to dig up two or three bushes so we can put the body in the hole. Then we'll replace the bushes so the ground looks just the way it did before."

"That's a good idea," said Hai. "But to do that, I will need someone stronger than you to help me. I will ask one of my friends."

Hai went to a friend who lived nearby. After swearing the friend to secrecy, Hai whispered the story in his ear. When he had finished, the man shook his head. "You know what a dear friend you are to me, Hai," he said. "But what you are asking is dangerous. It is against the law to hide a death. You are asking me to break the law. You and your wife should go to the mandarin and tell him the truth."

Hai went to the house of another friend, where he got the same answer. In a short while, he visited every one of his friends. But every one of them refused to help him. At last, tired and depressed, he went home and told his wife that all his friends had deserted him.

"Hai," she said, "forget about your so-called friends. Ask your brother to help you."

"Ba?" he said. "I never did anything for him, so why should he do this for me?"

"Go and ask."

Hai went to his brother's hut and knocked.

Ba opened the door. "What brings you here?"

Hai explained everything. Before Hai could even ask, Ba offered his help. Ba went home with Hai to wait for nightfall. In the cover of darkness, Ba helped Hai and his wife carry the rolled-up mat with the body in it. The three dug a hole and lowered the mat into it. Finally they covered up the grave with bushes.

The next morning, the three of them were called to the mandarin's house. When they got there, they saw all the friends whom Hai had begged for help the night before.

"Who did you say murdered a man?" the mandarin asked Hai's friends.

They all pointed to Hai's wife.

"Who did you say asked you for help in burying a murdered body?"

They all pointed to Hai.

"And who did you say actually helped these two bury the body?"

The friends pointed to Ba. "I saw Ba go to Hai's house last evening," said one of them. "And I knew that Hai would never invite Ba unless he wanted him to do some unpleasant chore."

"The woman is guilty of murder," the mandarin said. "You, Hai and Ba, are guilty of **conspiracy** to hide a murder. I order the three of you to show us where you buried the body."

Hai and his wife and brother led everyone to the grave. The mandarin ordered his officers to **exhume** the body. When the officers unearthed the body and unrolled the mat, the onlookers gasped with surprise at what they saw.

It was the corpse of a large, black dog.

"What is the meaning of this?" the mandarin demanded.

Hai's wife stepped forward. "Please let me explain. You see, my husband has always been kind to his friends but unkind to his brother. He was convinced that his friends would stand by him through thick and thin. He never thought he'd need the love and loyalty of his brother. But I knew his brother was a better person than any of his friends."

"So far you have explained nothing," said the mandarin.

"For quite a while, I've been concerned about my husband's choice of friends. They seemed to appreciate Hai only for the things he gave them. I knew when my husband really needed them, they would not be supportive."

Hai's friends stood speechless as his wife glared at them. "However," she continued, "just telling my husband this did no good. I had to show him who really loved and cared about him."

The mandarin spoke up, "This still does not tell me why a dog is buried under your bushes."

"I'm getting to that," said Hai's wife. "Yesterday our dog died, and the idea struck me. I know it was crazy, but I proved my point. It's obvious that Ba is the only person my husband can truly depend upon."

Upon hearing this, Hai fell sobbing into his brother's arms. The mandarin dismissed everyone. Hai's friends crept out silently, hanging their heads in shame.

After that, Hai considered Ba not only a brother but also his friend. He shared the family's property and possessions with his brother. The two worked together to make the farm prosper even more than it had before. They shared everything—good times and bad times, sorrows and successes—and loved each other the way brothers should.

INSIGHTS

Vietnam was ruled by China from 111 B.C. to 938 A.D. Consequently, Vietnamese culture has been greatly influenced by Chinese behavior and thinking. This influence is especially noticeable in Vietnamese education, art, literature, ethics, and family relationships. The story of the two brothers reflects, in part, ancient Chinese beliefs about family relationships.

Confucius was a Chinese philosopher who lived from 551 to 478 B.C. He taught that the family is the core of society. Confucianists believe that the morals and values taught by the family are carried over to all other relationships a person might have—business, friendship, and so on. To many modern Vietnamese, family is still the center of a person's life. The morals and values taught by the family are the basis for all interactions with other people.

At the time of this story, the father was the head of the family. His word was followed by all family members, including his wife and children. The children were taught to obey and honor both parents, but the father always had the most authority. This authority over the children continued as long as the father lived.

Sons were valued more than daughters. A son's privileges and rights were ranked according to his age. The oldest son was first in line to inherit the family fortune. Then he could decide how to share it with his other siblings.

Daughters' standings were ranked according to age also. But since males were valued more than females, the youngest son outranked even the eldest daughter.

Hai's wife, who dares tell him he's wrong and then proves it in public, might not be the model wife by traditional Vietnamese standards. Her character may reflect a more modern view of a woman's role.

A · S · I · A · N

FRIENDS AND NEIGHBORS

A Friend's Gift

The Good Couple and Their Bad Neighbors

Heng and Yong

Everyone searches for a true friend—someone who can be counted on in any situation. Cultures may differ in some aspects, but they probably all agree on the qualities a good friend should possess. And most cultures use myths to teach such qualities as loyalty, trust, and compassion.

The following tales are about friendship. As you read these stories, decide which of the characters you would want to have as friends.

M · Y · T · H · S

A FRIEND'S GIFT

VOCABULARY PREVIEW

The following words appear in the story. Review the list and get to know the words before you read the story.

bitterly—angrily; unkindly
charity—kindness; generosity
clerical—secretarial; office job
commotion—loud disturbance; disorder
confidently—surely; sure of success
humiliated—embarrassed
impatient—restless; eager
indignation—anger; resentment
inherited—received property after a relative's death
magistrate—judge
menial—common; low-paying
prestige—status; respect
privileged—one with many opportunities and rights; upper class
reminiscing—remembering; recalling
resigned—quit; gave up
sprawling—vast; stretched out

Main Characters

Luu Binh—wealthy scholar; Duong Le's friend
Duong Le—poor scholar; Luu Binh's friend
Chau Long—innkeeper

Sometimes friendship isn't what you expect it to be, as Luu Binh discovers in this tale.

A Friend's Gift

Adapted from a Vietnamese tale

Duong Le[1] and Luu Binh[2] had been friends since they were children. They studied together—and played pranks together—at the village school. And they had the same goal. Each boy wanted to become a mandarin—a highly respected government official. As a mandarin, a man could live a good life.

---

[1] (dwong lā)
[2] (lū bin yə)

However, anyone wishing to be a mandarin had to take a test called a civil service exam. This was a very difficult test, because not just anyone could become a mandarin. A man had to devote all of his time to prepare for it, which meant he could not have a job. This was not a problem for Luu Binh. He had **inherited** a small fortune from his father and did not have to work for a living. Duong Le, however, came from a poor family. His parents could no longer afford to let him live at home without paying for his room and board. Duong Le would have to work for a living. Because of this, he couldn't spend the entire day studying for the exam as Luu Binh could.

One afternoon Duong Le said to Luu Binh, "You and I have come to a parting of the ways. You will pass the examination and become a member of the **privileged** class. I, on the other hand, will go through life as a common laborer."

Luu Binh answered, "No, my friend, I can't allow that to happen. You must come and live in my house until the test is given again. The next exam is two years away. That gives us plenty of time to study, and we'll both pass. Then you'll never have to worry about money again." When Duong Le protested, Luu Binh said warmly, "In the name of true friendship, you must let me do this for you."

So Duong Le moved into Luu Binh's house. The two immediately began their studies for the difficult exam. As schoolboys, they had already memorized several books of Chinese literature. Now they studied other books and practiced their writing skills. They would spend hours discussing a difficult question or debating current issues.

At first both young men worked steadily from morning until night. But soon Luu Binh got tired of working so hard. One day in the middle of studying, he sat back in his chair. "We shouldn't have to kill ourselves to pass this exam," he said to Duong Le. "In fact, I'll bet we'll do better if we take a little rest every now and then. Come on, let's go get something to eat."

"You go ahead," Duong Le answered. "I can't spare the time. I have to finish memorizing this poem."

"You work too hard," argued Luu Binh. "It isn't necessary."

"To me, it is. I have to pass the exam the first time I take it. If I fail, there'll be no second chance for me. I'll have to get a **menial** job or go hungry. I certainly can't continue living on your **charity**."

"You worry too much. We'll both pass easily, you'll see."

This conversation ended with Duong Le staying in his room and Luu Binh going out to find entertainment. For the rest of the two years, Duong Le studied constantly, and Luu Binh studied when he felt like it.

On the appointed day, the two friends reported to the government building for the exam. Hundreds of other young men were there also. Guards searched each candidate for hidden notes. Then each man was locked in a small cell. The room was very quiet except for an occasional cough. Anyone who attempted to communicate with his neighbor was given an immediate failing grade.

After the test, everyone nervously awaited the results. "How did it go?" asked Duong Le.

"It was difficult. There were many things I didn't know," answered Luu Binh.

"Now comes the hardest part—waiting for the results. I'm sure you did fine, Luu Binh."

When the test papers were graded and the scores announced, Duong Le's name was on the short list of those who had passed. He received his degree and a mandarin's post in another province. Luu Binh's name was not on the list. He had failed.

Luu Binh was not only disappointed but **humiliated**. His friend tried to comfort him. "Never mind," Duong Le said. "You don't need a degree anyway. You have enough money to live comfortably without working. Besides, if you want a degree just for the **prestige** it brings, you can always take the exam again."

After Duong Le left to take up his new post, Luu Binh felt lonely. Of course he had many other friends, but they only liked him because he knew how to have a good time. Duong Le, by contrast, had appreciated Luu Binh's more serious talents. So Luu Binh decided to follow his friend's suggestion and take the examination again.

However, he still lacked the self-discipline to study. The exam was another three years away, so he told himself that two years of studying would be plenty. He could afford to relax and enjoy life for a few months.

After the twelve months were up, Luu Binh began his studies. But as before, he found it impossible to make himself work steadily every day. He took time off now and then for dining with his friends, going to the theater, and playing games of chance. As the months passed, he spent less and less time studying and more and more time amusing himself.

When only three months remained before the examination, Luu Binh finally faced reality. He had spent his entire fortune and gambled himself into debt. This time around, he simply had to pass the exam. So he closed himself in his room and forced himself to study.

However, his efforts were too little, too late. He failed the test for a second time.

For a few days he felt very sorry for himself. But finally he accepted his situation. He sold his house and everything in it, including all of his books. Then he paid off his debts. He rented a cheap room that was dark and cramped. Then he found a clerking job in the village **magistrate's** office. But the work was boring and paid poorly. "Well," he said to himself, "I didn't end up as a common laborer as Duong Le feared he would. But sometimes I think this is almost as bad."

Luu Binh's life sank into a dull, unsatisfying routine. As he worked, his mind often wandered to the happier days of the past. He thought about Duong Le and wondered how he was doing. He wondered even more about what Duong Le would think if he knew what had happened to his old friend.

Then one day Luu Binh had a daring thought. "I'll go to Duong Le and ask him for a job. Even though it will only be a lowly **clerical** position, at least I'd be working for Duong Le. I'll be treated like an old friend. We'll spend hours discussing literature and grand ideas. It will be like old times!"

Luu Binh packed his few belongings and left for the city where Duong Le served as mandarin. He was so sure that Duong Le would welcome him that he **resigned** his position at the magistrate's office.

When he arrived in the city, Luu Binh took a room at an inn and found out where Duong Le lived. He rested that night. The next morning, he made his way to Duong Le's house.

When Luu Binh arrived at Duong Le's beautiful house, a guard answered his knock. But the guard looked him over suspiciously. Luu Binh explained that he was an old friend of the mandarin. "You'll have to speak to His Lordship's secretary," the guard said gruffly.

Inside Luu Binh greeted the secretary politely and introduced himself. The secretary, who could tell by Luu Binh's clothing that he had no official rank, seemed **impatient**. "His Lordship is very busy," he said coldly. "Please state your business."

"Please tell him I'm in need of a job and have experience as a clerk," said Luu Binh. It was embarrassing for him to have to tell the secretary that he came in search of such a lowly position. "I would be grateful to have any position, no matter how humble."

"Wait here," the secretary said and walked away.

In a few minutes he was back. "His Lordship says he doesn't know any Luu Binh."

"What?" said Luu Binh. "There must be some mistake. We were schoolboys together. We studied for the civil service examination together!"

"You are mistaken. His Lordship has never heard of you."

"Let me talk to him," demanded Luu Binh, raising his voice.

The secretary took Luu Binh's arm and tried to steer him toward the door. But Luu Binh shook him off roughly. "If Duong Le saw me, he would remember me right away. I know he would!"

The guard heard the **commotion** and rushed into the room. He helped the secretary drag Luu Binh into the street. There the two gave Luu Binh a shove that sent him **sprawling** in the dust.

Luu Binh was trembling with shock and **indignation** as he struggled to his feet and brushed himself off. How could Duong Le insult his old friend in such an outrageous manner? There was no excuse for it. It was beyond belief.

Luu Binh slowly walked back to the inn, muttering **bitterly** to himself all the way. "So that's how he treats his oldest and best friend! If it weren't for me, he wouldn't be where he is today."

Kicking a stone down the street, he grew more upset as he thought about it. "That's gratitude for you! And that's the educated man for you! Educated man, ha! Duong Le knows the Book of Classic Poetry by heart, but he can't remember his friend's name! A learned man is supposed to be honorable, just, humble, and kind. Duong Le, the learned man. Ha!"

At the inn, Luu Binh made arrangements to leave right away. He knew he must get home and try to get his old job back before they hired somebody else.

As he was gathering his belongings, a refined-looking young woman came to his door and asked to speak with him. "I am Chau[3] Long, the landlady of this inn," she said.

"I am Luu Binh, your humble guest."

"I understand that you are a scholar," said Chau Long.

Luu Binh gave a short laugh. "A failed scholar," he answered. "I have taken the civil service test twice and failed it twice."

"Would you like to try again?" she asked.

"Yes, but unfortunately I have no time to study. I am poor and must work for a living."

[3] (chau)

"Suppose I let you stay in this inn free of charge. You could then devote your time to study."

"But why should you do such a thing for me?"

Chau Long bowed her head and seemed to wipe a tear from her eye. "My young son was on his way to becoming a premier scholar, but he died. I want to honor his memory by helping another scholar succeed."

"That's most generous of you. I don't know what to say."

"You need say nothing. Save your energy for studying. You will have a place to sleep and food to eat. If you're in need of a book, let me know and I'll bring it from my son's library."

"How can I ever repay you?" said Luu Binh, with tears in his eyes. "I thought I'd never have another chance, but you are giving me one. I'll be grateful to you for the rest of my life."

"You never need to repay me, just pass the test."

This time, Luu Binh was determined to pass. There was only a year and a half to get ready for the exam. But he resolved not to waste a minute of it. Every morning he got up early and worked until dark. He stopped only long enough to eat, and sometimes he even forgot to do that.

From time to time Chau Long would check on him. She usually insisted that he rest for a while. "You are working too hard," she would say. "There's no sense in killing yourself."

Luu Binh would laugh at this. One day he replied, "That's just what I used to say to a former friend of mine. Luckily for him, he was too smart to listen to me." He would continue to pore over his books.

At last the day of the examination arrived. Luu Binh answered all the questions easily and **confidently**. Even before the results were announced, he felt sure he had passed. When the list of successful candidates was published, Luu Binh's name was at the very top!

Eager to share his triumph with the person who had made it possible, Luu Binh rushed to the inn. He asked for

Chau Long, but nobody had seen her for several days. Then he asked when she might be expected to return. Finally one of the kitchen boys answered, "You've been her guest for so long, you know more about her comings and goings than we do."

That was the only response he got. And the puzzling reply discouraged Luu Binh from asking any more questions. Each day he continued to check at the front desk for Chau Long. One day as he passed, there was a letter waiting for him.

Delight showed on Luu Binh's face as he read the letter. He was appointed to an important position in the capital. He put off leaving the inn as long as he could, hoping that Chau Long would appear. But she never did. So he wrote a letter expressing his deep appreciation and left it for her. Then he set out for the capital to begin his new life as a mandarin.

Several years went by. One day, while traveling on official business, Luu Binh happened to be close to the home of Duong Le. Although he no longer considered the man his friend, he decided to pay him a call. He was curious to see how Duong Le would receive him.

The same guard and the same secretary were there. However, this time both treated Luu Binh with the utmost respect. When Luu Binh's name was announced, Duong Le hurried out to greet him and led him into a private sitting room. Both were acting as if the earlier visit hadn't happened. They were sipping tea and **reminiscing** about the old days at the village school when a woman brought in some refreshments. Luu Binh stared at her in amazement.

"I know you. You're the missing mistress of the inn!" exclaimed Luu Binh.

"This is my wife, Chau Long," said Duong Le.

"Your wife?" stammered Luu Binh. "But I thought . . . that is, I'm sure she said . . ."

Duong Le laughed. "I don't blame you for being confused. Chau Long, would you explain everything?"

"You see," Chau Long said, "when you came to see

Duong Le six years ago, he wanted to help you. But he knew it wouldn't really be helping if you were given the kind of job you were seeking. That would have left you in an inferior position for the rest of your life. He wanted more for you. Duong Le wanted you to pass the examination and become a mandarin. That is why he insulted you and turned you away."

"I was very hurt by that," said Luu Binh.

"It was painful for you both. But then Duong Le gave you a chance at a much better life by paying your room and board at the inn and lending his books to you. The rest was up to you, and you succeeded brilliantly."

"Then, that story about your son and his books . . . ?"

"I made that up," said Chau Long with a smile.

Luu Binh smiled back at her and said, "You gave a most convincing performance." He turned to Duong Le. "I must ask you the question I asked Chau Long six years ago: How can I ever thank you?"

"You don't have to thank me," answered Duong Le. "Remember all those years ago when you gave me room, board, and books? You made it possible for me to study for the exam. I only did for you what you had already done for me."

There was silence in the room for a few moments. Then Luu Binh said, "You have given me another gift today."

"What is that?" asked Duong Le.

"You have given me back the friend I thought I'd lost. To know that we're still friends and will always be friends makes me very happy."

"I understand," said Duong Le. "It makes me very happy too."

INSIGHTS

The coastal country of Vietnam was ruled by China for more than a thousand years, from 111 B.C. to 939 A.D. During that time, Chinese was the official language. Even after Vietnam won its independence from China, government documents and most literary works continued to be written in Chinese. This strong Chinese influence continued until the early 18th century.

Along with their language, the Chinese rulers brought their system of education and their method of choosing public officials. These traditions, too, lived on in Vietnam after independence.

Chinese education is based on the philosophy of Confucius (551–478 B.C.). Confucius believed that the purpose of education is to build strong moral character. This explains why the two students in the story had to master works of literature, philosophy, ethics, history, and poetry.

Confucius further believed that good government depends on the moral character of the ruler and all other public officials. When the emperor is wise, just, and kind, the people obey the laws willingly, and order is maintained. The proper education, Confucius taught, can help produce leaders who possess these virtues.

The examination system was a natural outgrowth of this philosophy of government and education. It began in 124 B.C. when Emperor Han Wu Ti[1] decided that his administrators should be experts in the Confucian classics. He set up examinations to test candidates on their knowledge of these classics. He also set up an academy where promising scholars were trained for high positions.

[1] (hän wü tē)

In both China and Vietnam, the examination system gave men of the lower classes a chance to improve their position in life. Of course, preparing for the examination was harder for a poor man like Duong Le than it was for the sons of prosperous families. But once a man passed the test, his chances for advancement were more or less equal to anyone else's.

The title Premier Scholar was given to men of outstanding intellect. Usually the title was awarded to men who placed first in the national examination. A few men, however, were given the title by the Emperor of Vietnam. Premier Scholar Hien,[2] who lived in the 13th century, was one of these. He earned the title by helping his ruler solve a riddle sent by the Mongolian Emperor of China.

[2] (hī´ yen)

THE GOOD COUPLE AND THEIR BAD NEIGHBORS

VOCABULARY PREVIEW

The following words appear in the story. Review the list and get to know the words before you read the story.

acquire—gain; get
aroma—pleasant smell; pleasing odor
desperation—loss of hope; madness
dismayed—alarmed; concerned
entrails—intestines; guts
groped—explored; felt
hoisted—lifted; raised
mallet—club; bat
millet—grain
miraculously—amazingly; surprisingly
paltry—small; worthless
ponder—think about; question
province—kingdom; territory
reverberated—vibrated; resonated
reverently—respectfully; solemnly
stench—bad smell; stink
tormented—agonized; afflicted
vile—disgusting; repulsive
yelp—cry; bark

Main Characters

good old couple—kind, generous husband and wife
bad old couple—greedy, cruel husband and wife

From swarming bees to a handmill that pours out rotten garbage— find out how the good couple's blessings become the bad couple's nightmares.

The Good Couple and Their Bad Neighbors

Retold from a Japanese tale

On the mountainside in the Koshu[1] **province**, there once lived a kindly old man and his kindly old wife. They lived very simply in a small thatched hut. They ate **millet** and fish because rice and meat were too expensive. The couple grew vegetables in a tiny garden behind their house. Not far from the house was a clear mountain stream where the old man often caught fish. Higher up the slope were forests full of deer, wild pigs, pheasants, and other animals. Rice paddies were terraced[2] into the mountainsides below the couple's hut. And nestled deep in the valley were more rice paddies.

[1] (kō´ shü)
[2] A paddy is a wet field or area where rice is grown. Paddies are often cut horizontally into the sloping sides of hills and mountains.

The kind old couple was poor, yet they never failed to share what little they had with others. But this was not true of the couple's neighbors. On the hill just below them lived another elderly couple. These two were continually asking for a loan or a gift. However, they would never think of offering a loan or gift to anyone else.

One evening, the two old men happened to meet at the stream. Each man set a fish trap, called a *do,*[3] and left it overnight in the water to catch fish.

Early the next morning, the lazy old man from the lower house checked his do. As he slowly **hoisted** it out of the water, he noticed a pair of big ears inside the crate. The farther he pulled it from the water, the furrier the creature got. He realized it was a puppy. It gulped in air and let out a loud **yelp**.

"How did you get in there?" he asked in a disapproving tone. The puppy just looked at him and wagged its tail.

"What good is a puppy?" he muttered to himself. "One end wags to win your heart, but the other end eats. What's worse, a small puppy grows into a big dog that eats even more."

He then raised his neighbor's do and opened it. It was overflowing with fish. "Why should he have all these good fish while I have none?" he thought. "It's not fair. However, I'll soon put things right."

The bad old man put all of his neighbor's fish into his own do. Then he put the puppy inside his neighbor's do. As he lowered the do back into the water, the puppy drew in a big breath. Then the bad old man took the stolen fish back to his house and gave them to his wife.

Later that day, the good old man from the upper house went to check his do. He was delighted to find the playful little puppy inside. "I have a feeling that you will bring us luck, little friend," he said, patting the puppy on the head. He dried the puppy's wet fur with his sleeve and carried it home.

When the good old man showed the unusual catch to

[3] (dōh)

his wife, she was also delighted. The couple fed the puppy—first from a cup, then from a bowl, and finally from a pot. Within a few months it became a full-grown mountain dog. This dog was unusually large and unusually smart. It easily learned to carry tools and other loads on its back. And it had a special talent for catching deer in the mountains.

One morning, when the good old man and his dog were hunting deer, the bad old man happened to come along and spot them. He hid behind a tree and watched to see what would happen. He heard the good old man give a command to the dog, "My good dog without any fear, go look and search and bring me deer."

The man and his dog were in a small clearing. The dog trotted around the edge of the clearing, barking softly as he went. Immediately, deer poured out of the woods. The dog picked out several of the largest and chased them down. Quickly and easily, the dog caught the chosen deer, and each fell to the ground. Then the good old man loaded the deer onto the dog's back and went home.

Tormented by envy, the bad old man walked home muttering, "That dog should have been mine. It is a magical dog. The gods must have put him in my trap. I would never have traded it for a few **paltry** fish had I known it was a magical dog. It's just my luck to be cheated by that crafty old man in the upper house!" By the time the bad old man got home, he was convinced that he was the rightful owner of the magical dog. His wife agreed with him, of course.

That evening, while the good couple and their dog were enjoying a delicious deer stew, the woman from the lower house dropped by. "I hate to disturb you," she said, "but the wonderful smell of your stew is drifting down the hill to our house. My husband told me about that deer-catching dog of yours. Oh, how we'd love to eat deer stew too! Could we possibly borrow your dog for a day, just long enough to catch some deer for ourselves?"

The kind couple said yes, not even pausing to **ponder** such a generous act. "Be good to our neighbor," said the good old man to the dog.

The woman led the dog home, but she didn't want it in her house. And she couldn't leave it outside for fear it would run away. So she shut the dog in a small shed.

The next day, the man from the lower house took the dog to the same spot where he had spied on his neighbor the day before. Standing in the clearing, he shouted, "Dog, now move a little faster, bring a prize for your new master!"

The dog trotted around the edge of the clearing, barking as before. But this time, no deer came out of the woods. Instead, swarms of angry bees appeared from every direction. Hundreds of them flew straight to the bad old man, settled on his face, neck, and arms, and stuck their stingers into him. Every time he managed to brush some away, others attacked him. Screaming at the top of his lungs, the bad old man stumbled around the clearing.

As quickly as the bees had appeared, they flew away. When the bees had gone, the injured man stopped to check his wounds. Every bit of skin he could see was covered with red splotches that burned like fire. In a rage he picked up a large stick that was lying nearby and started to beat the dog. "You miserable dog!" he shouted. "It's all your fault! You were supposed to bring me deer, but instead you brought bees." He was so furious that he hit the animal again and again. Suddenly, the dog turned to stone. The man's hand and arm **reverberated** with every blow. He was astonished by the dog's transformation.

Back in the upper house, the kind couple waited all day for the return of their beloved pet. Toward evening they were **dismayed** to see the bad old man returning with blisters all over his face and neck but without their dog.

"Look what your dog did to me!" the bad old man said bitterly. "When I told him to bring me deer, he stirred up a nest of bees that practically killed me with their poisonous stings."

"I am sorry to see you in such pain," said the good old man. "But where is our dog?"

"The bees stung him too, and he died," lied the bad old man. "I buried him in a nearby rice field under a cherry tree."

The couple wept when they heard that their dear friend was dead. But they generously gave the bad old man one of the deer that the dog had caught the day before. "Please take this gift since we are to blame for your misfortune," they told him.

The next day, the good old man went to the rice field where the dog was buried. He found the cherry tree that marked his devoted friend's grave and cut it down. Then he made a handmill out of the beautiful wood. As soon as it was finished, the man's wife set the handmill on the floor and began to turn the handle. As she worked she sang, "Help us work and help us grind, dear friend our handmill, true and kind."

Suddenly rice began pouring out of the mill. It spilled out onto the floor, and the couple joyfully gathered it up and put it into a large bowl. After that they filled a larger bowl and after that a basket. Still the rice kept coming. As long as the good old woman turned the handle of the mill, the rice kept streaming out. It came in such great amounts every day that the good couple had much more rice than they needed. They began to sell it, and soon they became very wealthy.

Once again the bad couple was jealous of their neighbors' success. So they went to the kind couple and asked how they had managed to **acquire** such wealth. The good couple showed their neighbors the handmill and explained how it had made them rich.

"You must lend us this handmill," the couple from the lower house said. "We would like to get rich too."

"You are welcome to borrow it," said the good couple.

When they got home, the bad couple started grinding the handmill as hard as they could. As they worked, they sang, "Handmill, give us lots of treasure, without limit, without measure."

Suddenly something began pouring out of the handmill. But it was not rice or any other treasure. It was a **vile** green slime dotted with chunks of putrid meat, rotten eggs, fish **entrails**, moldy bamboo shoots, and other disgusting bits of garbage. It filled the entire house with an awful **stench**. Although the couple immediately stopped grinding the mill, the stream of decaying matter kept flowing out. Finally, in **desperation**, the bad old man seized an ax, split the handmill in two, and threw it into the fire.

The next day the greedy couple returned the handmill to its owners in the form of ashes. "You should have warned us that the handmill was not to be trusted," said the bad old man.

"Yes," said his wife. "It is not fair that the handmill gave you rice but gave us a stinking mess of garbage stew. We couldn't get it to stop."

After the kind old couple had given them a large basket of rice to make up for their trouble, the bad couple left. Then the good old man said to his wife, "I think we should honor our friend the handmill by scattering its ashes in the garden." His wife agreed, so the two of them **reverently** carried the ashes out to the garden. The man tossed some of the ashes into the wind and said, "Go and blow, oh, wind so strong, and find the place where these belong."

Some geese just happened to be flying overhead. All at once, a blast of wind blew the ashes straight up into the geese's eyes. **Miraculously** the birds fell dead onto the ground. The kind couple was delighted at this. Goose was a delicacy compared to their typical rice and millet diet. They carried the birds into their house and prepared a fine meal of grilled goose.

Soon the mouthwatering **aroma** of goose drifted from the upper house down to the nostrils of the bad couple. They could not resist going to the upper house to find out what smelled so delicious. The kind couple told them what had happened after they scattered the ashes.

"Are there any ashes left?" asked the greedy couple.

"Why, yes," said the good old woman. "There is at least a handful."

"In that case," the greedy couple said, "you must give them to us. We want to eat grilled goose too."

The good couple gave the bad couple what was left of the ashes.

When the bad couple got home, the old man leaned a ladder against the roof and climbed up to the top. There he tossed the ashes into the air and said, "Obey me, ashes, go and serve, and give me all that I deserve."

Suddenly the wind shifted and blew the ashes right back into the old man's face. The ashes went into his eyes, blinding him. As he **groped** around for the ladder, he lost his balance, slid down the roof, and tumbled to the ground. His wife, who was inside the house getting her pots and pans ready, heard the fuss. She ran outside waving a **mallet** above her head. In her haste, she did not see her husband lying on the ground. As she ran by him, he grabbed her foot. This startled her so that she beat him on the head. The man was out cold before she realized who he was.

After that the bad couple stopped bothering the kind old couple who lived in the upper house. You might conclude from this that the bad couple mended their ways. Sad to say, however, your conclusion would be wrong. What happened was that the bad couple met another couple who was just as bad as they were. The two bad couples then began to play an endless game of cheating one another, and this took up all their time. So the good old man and his wife were free of their pesky neighbors at last.

INSIGHTS

The good old man and the bad old man are characters in many Japanese tales. Another tale in which these characters appear is about a rich farmer and a poor farmer who were neighbors. One day Buddha, disguised as a beggar, asked for a night's lodging at the rich man's house. The greedy rich man refused the god with harsh words. When Buddha went next door to the poor farmer, he was warmly welcomed.

The next morning, Buddha revealed his identity. He then planted a tree in front of the house, telling the poor old farmer to make anything he wished from it. The tree grew rapidly. The poor farmer cut it down and made a mortar and pestle from the wood. After he put a small amount of rice into the mortar, huge quantities of rice flowed endlessly.

Witnessing this, the greedy rich farmer borrowed the mortar and pestle. But it did the reverse for him. The rice actually disappeared as he put it into the mortar.

In most stories, the good characters are compassionate and generous in spite of their poverty. This is a value taught in Buddhism, a national religion in Japan since 700 A.D. Today, there are approximately fifty million practicing Japanese Buddhists. Buddhists believe suffering is a part of life. The only way a person can avoid suffering is by giving up all worldly desires. To Buddhists, compassion is an essential virtue. A compassionate person tries to free all life from suffering.

The poor farmer has compassion for the man he believes is a beggar. The good couple in the upper house practice an even more demanding kind of compassion. They have compassion for those who don't deserve it.

---

[1] (buhd´ a) Buddha, "enlightened one," is the title given to Siddhartha Gautama of India, who achieved status around the world as a spiritual leader and teacher. He is the most important god in the Buddhist religion.

The bad couple kill the good couple's dog and burn their handmill. But the good couple never seek revenge. They are willing to continue helping the bad couple.

These stories also reflect a respect for nature that is part of both Buddhism and Shintoism.[2] Shintoism was the first religion in Japan. Shintoists pray to natural deities, such as the sun god. Shintoism suggests that everything in the world has a spirit, or *kami*.[3] The kami remains even when the object changes from one form to another.

For example, both of our stories involve a tree. In the story about the two couples, it's a cherry tree, one of the best-loved trees in Japan. The tree is cut down, and some of its wood is made into a handmill. The kami of the tree is in the handmill. Later, when the handmill is burned, the kami is in the ashes. That is why both the handmill and the ashes have the power to perform good deeds for the benefit of the good couple.

---

[2] (shin´ tō izm) Shintoism is the ancient religion of Japan. It involves paying reverence to ancestors and natural spirits.
[3] (ka´ mē) A *kami* is a spirit of nature in the Shinto religion.

HENG AND YONG

VOCABULARY PREVIEW

The following words appear in the story. Review the list and get to know the words before you read the story.

accustomed—in the habit of; used to
compensate—make up for; balance
contritely—regretfully
frequently—often; regularly
gracious—generous; kind
impose—interfere; cause hardship
lingered—remained; lasted
peddler—salesman; vendor
prosperous—successful; rich
solemn—serious; sacred
succulent—juicy; fresh
sympathetically—with caring and understanding; kindly
tattered—worn out; torn
wharves—ocean docks used to load and unload ships

Main Characters

Heng—peddler
Yong—dock worker

We all would like our lives to be rich and fulfilling. But how much should we be willing to sacrifice to meet our goals? Heng and Yong find out in this folktale.

Heng & Yong

Adapted from a Thai folktale

Two young men named Heng and Yong lived in a southern Chinese village. One year the rice crop failed, and the villagers had barely enough food to eat. So the two friends decided to leave the tiny village and find their fortunes. However, neither was sure just how to go about it.

"I once heard two merchants talking about trade ships sailing from China," said Yong. "Maybe we could find our fortunes as ship workers."

"Working on a ship won't make us wealthy men," said Heng. "We must build our own businesses to become rich. I've heard that there are such opportunities in Bangkok[1] for one who is willing to work hard."

"But how do we get to the city of Bangkok?" wondered Yong. "It's very far away, and we have no money for the journey."

---

[1] (bän´ käk) Bangkok is the capital of Thailand.

Heng thought about the question and finally answered, "We'll get jobs on a ship that goes to Bangkok. That way we can pay for passage with our labor."

And that's just what they did. After several days at sea, Heng and Yong arrived in Bangkok eager to become **prosperous** businessmen.

"How do you plan to make your fortune?" Yong asked his friend as they walked from the boat.

"I believe I'll start out as a **peddler**," answered Heng. "What will you do?"

"The only thing I know how to do is carry things," said Yong. "So I guess I'll try to get work on the **wharves**."

Heng nodded. "Well, the city is so large that we may not see each other for a while. But before we part, I have a suggestion. To save money, let's make a **solemn** vow not to eat pork or duck until we have made at least five hundred ticals."[2]

"Yes," Yong agreed. "This vow will make us both rich men someday." The two men shook hands and departed.

As soon as he could, Heng set himself up as a peddler. At first he sold small, inexpensive items, such as soap, thread, needles, candles, combs, and matches. He worked hard and saved his money from the first day. He stuck to his vow and ate only rice, vegetables, and noodles.

Before long, Heng was able to add cloth, baskets, and porcelain[3] dishes to his wares. He continued to save his money and eventually had enough to open a store. When the business prospered and he had well over five hundred ticals, he furnished the second floor of his shop and got married. Finally he was able to eat pork, duck, fish, and eggs whenever he wanted.

For the first two weeks after the friends separated, Yong also stuck to his vow. He worked hard and saved money by eating only rice, vegetables, and noodles. But the roast ducks he saw hanging in the shops along the wharf each day were extremely tempting.

---

[2] (ti´ käls) A *tical* is a silver coin worth about 60 cents. The currency was used in Siam until 1928 when it was replaced by the baht (bat).
[3] (pōr´ sə lən) Porcelain is a material used to make fine china.

One day, he couldn't resist any longer. "Just this once," he told himself. "I will eat duck tonight and go back to my solemn vow tomorrow."

Yong bought a duck and had a delightful, satisfying dinner. He slept soundly that night. When he woke up the next morning, the taste of roast duck still **lingered** in his mouth. All day long as he bent under his heavy load, he thought about the duck. He remembered the spicy aroma, the **succulent** meat, and the crispy skin of the duck.

On the way home that evening, he bought another duck. Once again he told himself that this would be the last one until he had more than five hundred ticals. But the next day, Yong's craving for duck was even more intense. From that day on, he **frequently** ate duck. He didn't forget his promise, but he continued to break it.

Since all of his money was spent buying meat, Yong remained poor. He often wondered whether his friend Heng had a better life than he did. Finally he decided to pay Heng a visit and find out.

Yong inquired about his friend in a shop that sold cloth, pots and pans, knives, and other household goods. "Do you know where a peddler named Heng lives?" he asked. He was quite surprised when he was directed to a big shophouse in an orchard. On the lower floor, he found his friend. Heng, dressed in fine clothes, was talking to a group of customers. Yong felt embarrassed because his own clothes were **tattered** and dirty.

Heng greeted him warmly. "How wonderful to see you, Yong!" he exclaimed. "You must stay and have dinner with me. I want to tell you about my life and find out about yours."

Yong accepted the invitation. As they ate Yong explained to Heng why he had not been able to save any money. "I can't bear to go through day after day of back-breaking labor without giving myself a few small pleasures," he said.

Heng nodded **sympathetically**. "If you like, you may live here," he said. "That way, you'll have no living expenses, and you will soon save enough money to have a comfortable life."

"Thank you for the invitation, but won't I **impose**?"

"It's no imposition. We have a small hut among the tamarind⁴ trees. You may stay in it. My wife will send you rice and salted fish for your meals. Pick just a few leaves from the smallest tamarind⁴ tree and boil them with your rice and fish. It will give them flavor."

Yong accepted his friend's **gracious** offer. The first few days went well. But then Yong began to miss the spicy duck to which he'd grown **accustomed**. To **compensate**, he generously seasoned his fish with tamarind. In a few days, Yong had picked all the leaves off the smallest tamarind tree. So he went to Heng to ask for permission to pick from another tree.

His friend chuckled. "Yong," he said, "what you have done to the tree is exactly what you have done to your own future. Instead of taking a few leaves at a time and letting new ones grow, you have stripped the leaves from the tree. In fact, you have probably killed it. Even if it lives, it will need time to grow new leaves.

"Likewise, instead of spending as little money as possible and saving the rest, you have spent all and saved nothing. Thus you have killed your chances of getting ahead."

"You are right," Yong replied **contritely**. "I will go back to my job on the wharf. I'll save money by eating only rice, vegetables, and noodles."

Heng gave him an encouraging smile. "Yes, that's what you should do. And you must come and have dinner with me once every week," he added kindly. "We'll feast on duck, pork, eggs—whatever you like."

This time Yong kept his promise. He went back to the wharf, worked hard, and saved his money. When Yong had enough, Heng helped him start a cargo boat business. After a few years, Yong owned a whole fleet of cargo boats. He too was a prosperous man.

---

⁴ (ta´ mə rənd) A tamarind tree has yellow bark, red and yellow flowers, and leaves resembling feathers. The flavorful leaves are often used as food seasonings.

INSIGHTS

Stories like "Heng and Yong" are quite common in Thailand, where the Chinese have been an important minority group for centuries.

In many Thai folktales, the Chinese are negatively portrayed as cunning businessmen or moneylenders who prosper at the expense of the simple Thai farmer. These types of stories reflect a resentment on the part of some Thais against the Chinese.

The prejudice stems from the fact that the majority of Thai businesses, factories, and banks are run by Chinese or people of Chinese descent. Some people complain that the Chinese have too much control over the nation's economy.

But the Chinese prominence in business is the natural result of two factors. First, the Thais have traditionally preferred agricultural work to any other kind. It is not surprising that the Chinese immigrants found their greatest opportunities in areas the Thais avoided.

Second, the Chinese are generally extremely hard workers. So both Thai and Chinese folktales have portrayed the Chinese as willing to endure great hardships.

Tales like "Heng and Yong" may give the impression that the Chinese and the Thais are two distinct groups. The fact is, however, that they are often hard to tell apart. Until quite recently, almost all Chinese immigrants were men, and most of these men married Thai women. It is said that after centuries of intermarriage, there are very few Thai citizens who do not have some Chinese blood in their veins.

The majority of the Chinese who settled in Bangkok were Teochius,[1] like Heng and Yong. They were encouraged to come by King Taksin,[2] who ruled Siam from 1768 to 1782. The king favored this group because his own father was a Teochiu.

[1] (tyaw chūs´)
[2] (tak´ sin)

A · S · I · A · N

SMART AND NOT-SO-SMART

Gold for the Clever Man

Monkey and Turtle

The Kind Fool

The art of tricking people is the focus of many myths and folktales. Tricksters represent the value a culture places on a cunning mind and clever wit.

Trickster tales often contain humorous characters. The most popular Asian tricksters are the monkey, the turtle, the deermouse, and children. These characters can be good or bad. Sometimes tricksters outsmart other people, and sometimes they are outsmarted. In each story in this section, the tricksters are fooled by someone wiser.

M · Y · T · H · S

GOLD FOR THE CLEVER MAN

VOCABULARY PREVIEW

The following words appear in the story. Review the list and get to know the words before you read the story.

appetizing—tasty; mouthwatering
bellowed—yelled; cried out
bore—gave; produced
chestnut—reddish brown
commenced—began; started
concocted—made up; dreamed up; thought up
contemptuously—insultingly; scornfully
courtiers—attendants; members of a royal court
despise—greatly dislike; hate
devotion—affection; love
embroidered—detailed with needlework
furor—commotion; fuss
gluttony—greed; being piggish
incredible—unbelievable; fantastic
promptness—being on time; punctuality
pungent—spicy or strong odor
regally—nobly; kingly
sages—wise ones
self-indulgence—pursuit of pleasure
subsiding—settling; decreasing
suspicions—distrust; doubts
verify—confirm
wit—intelligence; cleverness

Main Characters

king—ruler of Cochin
Kalloor—courtier
Dadhich—elderly courtier

On All Fools Day, anyone who could outsmart the king would win bags of gold. Of course the king never had to pay— until he met the clever man.

Gold for the Clever Man

Adapted from a tale from India

The streets of Cochin[1] were decorated with fragrant and colorful flowers. Women were in their kitchens preparing special dishes for a feast. Men rowed long, narrow snakeboats in preparation for the annual race. All the people were dressed in their finest outfits, for it was a special holiday—Vinayaka Chaturthi,[2] or All Fools Day.

One of the most popular events planned for this day was a liars' contest at the palace. The king, who considered himself a talented storyteller, also enjoyed a good tale. And what better way to celebrate All Fools Day than to fool the king! The king was sure he wouldn't have to award any prizes. No one had ever been able to fool him before.

---

[1] (kō´ chən) Cochin was once located on the Arabian seacoast in southwest India.

[2] (vēnä ya ka cha tərt´ hē) Vinayaka Chaturthi celebrates the birth of Ganesha, the elephant-headed god of wisdom and success.

The townspeople listened excitedly as the king announced the rules and prizes. "The three best liars in the kingdom will each receive a bag of gold," he proudly announced. "The first bag will go to the man who can tell a completely false tale and make us all believe it really happened. The second bag will go to the man who can convince us that a dish he tasted was the most delicious dish of the day. And the third bag will go to the man who can convince us that he is the luckiest man in the whole kingdom.

"Any man who wishes to enter the contest may do so," the king continued. "**Sages**, scholars, craftsmen, fishermen, farmers—all will be welcome. The only requirement is that he be good at telling lies." The king paused and glanced at the **courtiers** gathered around him. "I'm sure many of you are well-qualified to enter!" he said with half a smile.

All but one of the courtiers shuffled their feet and exchanged nervous looks. No one laughed until he was sure the king was joking.

The one courtier who was not nervous was a young man named Kalloor.[3] He now boldly spoke. "Your majesty, do you remember what the teacher said to King Bali[4] the Great?"

"No," answered the king in a deep voice. "What did he say?"

"He said it was all right for a man to tell falsehoods if he must do so to earn a living."

Other courtiers gasped. It was unheard of to speak directly to the king. But the king just threw back his head and laughed heartily. Then of course, everyone else laughed too. But even as the other courtiers laughed, they cast angry looks at Kalloor. The young man's **wit** had already made him a favorite with the king, and the others were jealous.

The contest was scheduled to begin when the morning sun peaked in the sky. Many contestants began arriving well before that time, for the king demanded **promptness**.

[3] (ka´ lur)
[4] (bul´ i) King Bali was a member of the race of Asuras. The word *Asuras* roughly translates to "demons." However, Bali was a kind ruler.

By midmorning, several men were already pacing up and down the banquet hall. They were muttering, waving their hands in the air, and striking poses. Some were preparing to tell of finding treasure in a mountain cave or outwitting a goblin. One was rehearsing a tale about a man-eating tiger. Another was practicing a story of winning the love of a princess although her father objected to their marriage. Still others planned stories of getting caught in a stampede of wild elephants or bringing home an old lamp with a genie in it. Everyone had an **incredible** adventure to tell about.

Several other men were staring at the food set out on the banquet table. Their minds were busy developing stories of the most delicious foods in the kingdom. They **concocted** mouthwatering descriptions of coconut chutney, spiced lamb, grilled prawns,[5] chicken curry, sweet carrot pudding, and other heavenly dishes. Some stories were real and some were imagined.

People of the kingdom anxiously gathered for the lying contest. All the king's subjects had been invited, and every inch of standing space from the banquet table to the door was filled.

When the sun reached its highest point, the king swept into the room. The courtiers, the contestants, and the onlookers bowed. The king nodded **regally** and sat on a throne placed on a low platform. Royal attendants set before him a table with three bags of richly **embroidered** cloth. The king nodded again, drew his breath, and opened his mouth to declare, "Let the competition begin."

But before the king could speak, an elderly courtier named Dadhich[6] cut him off. "Your Majesty," said Dadhich, "if it is not asking too much, would you mind counting the coins in each bag in full view of the townspeople gathered here?"

---

[5] A *prawn* is a seafood that resembles a shrimp.

[6] (dad´ hich)

Had it been any other day, the man would instantly have been chained and sent to the dungeon. But since it was a special occasion, the king kindly agreed. With a smile, he pulled out the coins from each bag, one at a time, and carefully counted them. There were exactly 101 coins in each bag.

Everyone clapped politely as the king refilled and retied the last bag. He smiled, nodded, and **commenced** to declare the contest open. But before he could speak, another voice cut him off.

"I beg your pardon, your majesty," the voice said. "I wasn't present when the coins were counted. May I see them counted once more?"

"Who dares interrupt me again?" the king **bellowed**, slamming his fist on the table.

"It is I, Kalloor."

Everyone stared at Kalloor as he came forward and stood before the king.

The king shook his head angrily. "It is enough that everyone here witnessed the counting. They can **verify** the amount. And besides, you are late! You know how much I **despise** latecomers. What is your excuse?"

"Well, Your Highness," Kalloor said, "I'm afraid I don't have a very good excuse. I ate too much for breakfast—that's all. To tell the truth, I was stuffed to the teeth. I just had to lie down to settle my stomach, and I fell asleep. By the time I awoke, it was almost time for the contest to begin. So I jumped up and rushed out of the house. I tried to run, but you know how hard it is to run on a full stomach."

"Bah, such **self-indulgence**!" said the king **contemptuously**. "If there's anything I despise more than tardiness, it's **gluttony**. Besides, how could you eat so much when you knew there would be a banquet waiting for you here?"

"Sire, my wife had prepared *pazha prathaman*,[7] and I just couldn't insult her by not eating any."

[7] (päz´ ha prät ha´ man) *Pazha prathaman* is banana pudding.

All this time, the jealous courtiers had been delighted over Kalloor's disgrace. But now it seemed that the king's anger was **subsiding**. Hoping to make it flare up again, one of the courtiers said to the king, "Bananas, your majesty? How could his wife get bananas? The monsoons came early this year and flooded the crops."

"Yes, Kalloor," said the king, his **suspicions** aroused. "No one else has bananas. How did yours manage to survive?"

Kalloor nodded. "Your majesty, our tree was brought down from the slopes of the Western Ghats.[8] It was so high there that the floods didn't touch the fields. You see, our daughter, who recently married and moved away, sent that tree to us from her new home. And my wife, who misses our daughter very much, loves that tree. She fusses and prays over it every day. So when it finally **bore** fruit, she cut the bunch down herself, all eighty-five golden bananas, and made the dish. How could a man fail to show his appreciation for such **devotion**?"

"You are quite right," agreed the king. "A loving husband does his best to eat his wife's cooking, whether it is **appetizing** or not."

"Oh, but it *was* appetizing," protested Kalloor. "My wife has her own special recipe, you see. She boils the finest molasses with water to make a rich **chestnut**-colored syrup. Then she cooks the bananas until they're soft and adds the syrup and some ghee.[9] Next she stirs in fresh milk from sun-ripened coconut meat and lets the mixture simmer. As the sweet aroma fills the house, she fries crunchy slices of coconut meat and **pungent** cumin[10] seeds and adds these to the pudding. What a combination of flavors and textures! It's soft and smooth, yet there's a touch of crispness in each taste. It's sweet and creamy, yet there's a hint of spice to tickle your tongue. In short, my wife's pazha prathaman is a dish fit for a king!"

"If that's the case," said one of the jealous courtiers, "you should have brought it here and presented it to the king, instead of gobbling it all up yourself."

[8] (gäts)
[9] (gē) *Ghee* is butter.
[10] (kə´ mən)

"Yes, yes," cried several others, "your behavior is an insult to the king!"

In the midst of the **furor**, Kalloor calmly walked to the table and picked up a bag of gold. The king glowered at him. "And what do you think you are doing?" he demanded.

Without batting an eyelash, Kalloor answered, "The story I have just told to explain my tardiness was pure invention. Not a word of it was true; yet you all believed me."

There was stunned silence. Nobody wanted to admit falling so completely into Kalloor's trap, but there was no way to deny it.

The king was the first to recover his good humor. He smiled at the young man and announced that Kalloor rightly deserved the first bag of gold. The audience burst into loud applause.

When the hall was quiet again, Kalloor reached out and took the second bag of gold.

"Now, what is this?" the king asked in surprise. "Why take the second bag?"

Kalloor replied, "Because I also convinced the entire assembly that I had tasted the most delicious dish of this day."

The king let out a roar of laughter. Nobody dared argue, for their mouths had watered as he described that most delicious dish to the king. This time the crowd's applause was even louder.

The noise had barely died down when Kalloor stepped up to the table once again and took the third bag of gold. Before anyone could protest, the young man spoke. "Surely, the man who has just won two bags of gold is the luckiest man of all!"

At this, the palace fairly rocked with cheers and laughter. Of course the jealous courtiers were not happy. But everyone else, from the king to the lowliest member of the kingdom, was well pleased with the morning's entertainment. As for the clever Kalloor, he was led home in a parade, tightly clutching his three bags of gold.

INSIGHTS

The kingdom of Cochin, where this story takes place, was once located in southwestern India on the coast of the Arabian Sea. Soon after India gained its independence in 1946, the kingdom ceased to exist. The territory, once ruled by the kings of Cochin, is now part of the state of Kerala.[1]

The holiday in this story is part of the festival of Onam,[2] which honors the legendary King Bali. This festival is the most important celebration of the year in Kerala. The people take part in solemn religious ceremonies. They also enjoy parties, feasts, games, and sports, such as the famous snakeboat races.

According to legend, Bali was a member of the race of Asuras,[3] or demons. In spite of his background, however, he was a kind ruler who was greatly loved by his people. There was peace, prosperity, and happiness everywhere in his kingdom.

If Bali had one fault, it was that he was too fond of power. He grew more and more powerful until finally he ruled earth, heaven, and the underworld. He even drove the god Indra[4] off his heavenly throne.

The other gods asked the great god Vishnu[5] to rid them of Bali. So Vishnu went to earth in the form of a dwarf and called himself Vamana.[6] Dressed as a priest, he went to Bali's palace for an important religious ceremony. On such an occasion, the laws of hospitality required that the

[1] (ker´ ə lə)
[2] (o´ nam)
[3] (us´ uh rus)
[4] (in´ dru) Indra was a minor god with evil characteristics.
[5] (vish´ nu) Vishnu is represented with four hands and blue skin. He is associated with sun and light.
[6] (vah´ mu nu) Vamana is the god of sky and water. He has supreme rule over matters of law and justice.

king give his guests anything they asked for. When Bali invited Vamana to make a request, Vamana replied, "O, King, all I want is the amount of land I can cover in three steps."

Bali laughed and told Vamana that he should ask for something more. Vamana replied that a wise man is content with little. At this point Bali's guru,[7] Sakhra,[8] tried to warn the king that he was about to be tricked. He advised the king to go back on his word and refuse to give Vamana what he asked for. He told Bali that, under the circumstances, his falsehood would be no sin. But Bali was too proud and too honorable to listen to Sakhra. The king granted Vamana's request.

No sooner was that done than the dwarf began to grow. He grew larger and larger until he was bigger than the tallest mountain. With his first step he covered the earth. With his second step he covered the heavens. And there was no place left for his third step!

By now, Bali knew that he was dealing with Vishnu. The king also knew that if he broke his promise, he would be cast into the underworld. So he said to Vishnu, "For your third step, place your foot on my head." Vishnu did so, and under the weight of the god's foot, Bali sank down into the underworld.

However, Vishnu was pleased by Bali's honesty. As a reward, he made Bali king of the demons in the underworld. He also gave Bali permission to visit the earth one day every year. Vishnu even gave Bali the title Mahabali,[9] which means Bali the Great.

Bali's earthly visit takes place on the second day of the Onam festival. The people prepare for it by cleaning their houses and decorating the streets with flowers. They place clay images of Vamana on their household altars. The oldest member of each family gives new clothes to the other members.

[7] (gur´ ü) A guru is a spiritual teacher of eastern religions.
[8] (säk´ ra)
[9] (mu hah´ bul i)

Vinayaka Chaturthi, which is called All Fools Day in the story, is much better known as the festival of Ganesha,[10] the elephant-headed god. Ganesha is the god of wisdom and success, the remover of obstacles. It is said that even the other gods have sometimes prayed to Ganesha.

Vishnu, for example, prayed to Ganesha for help in defeating Bali. With Ganesha's help, Vishnu overcame Bali by means of falsehood and trickery. Had Bali listened to Sakhra, his guru, he may have been leery of such tricks. So perhaps a liars' contest is a fitting way to celebrate the day.

[10] (gŭ nā´ shŭ)

MONKEY AND TURTLE

VOCABULARY PREVIEW

The following words appear in the story. Review the list
and get to know the words before you read the story.

astounded—surprised; amazed
baffled—confused; puzzled
dawned—occurred to; entered one's mind
delectable—tasty; delicious
frantically—wildly; excitedly
grieving—crying; sobbing
harvest—gather or pick a crop
indignantly—angrily; resentfully
mockingly—insultingly; scornfully
perplexed—puzzled; confused
retreated—pulled back; hid for safety
scoundrel—villain; good-for-nothing
smug—proud; vain; cocky
stumped—baffled; confused
suspiciously—distrustfully; suspectingly
withered—wilted; dried up from heat

Main Characters

Monkey—Turtle's friend
Turtle—Monkey's friend

Monkey & Turtle

Monkey and Turtle are friends—at least that's what they call themselves. But some people might describe their relationship in a different way.

Adapted from several Filipino tales

Monkey and Turtle were friends. They got along fine—except when they found something to quarrel about. And they trusted each other completely—until one thought the other was cheating.

One day the two friends were standing on the riverbank watching the water flow by. Suddenly Turtle spotted something snagged on some rocks at the water's edge.

"Look," he said to Monkey. "The river has left us a present. I wonder what it is?"

"I'll skip down there and find out," said Monkey.

"No you won't!" said Turtle. "We'll go together." Turtle thought this was a good time to keep an eye on his friend.

So together they inched down the bank at Turtle's speed. When they finally got close to the object, Monkey exclaimed, "Why, if it isn't a banana plant!"

"So it is," agreed Turtle. "And since I saw it first, it's mine. Mmm, I can already taste those sweet, **delectable** fruits!"

"What do you mean, it's yours?" said Monkey. "I was the one who first saw it. The plant should go to me."

Turtle sighed. "It's a pity there's only one plant, and there are two of us."

Monkey thought for a minute. Then he said, "I know! Let's cut the plant in two so we can each have half."

"Good idea," said Turtle.

So after carefully finding the middle of the plant, they cut the trunk in two. Then they laid the top and the bottom side by side and compared them.

"They're equal in size, all right," said Monkey, "but are they equal in value? They look quite different to me. The top half has leaves while the bottom half has roots." He looked at the two parts with a **perplexed** expression and scratched his head.

Turtle saw that Monkey didn't know which half of the plant was the better half. So he said slyly, "Yes, I'm afraid we still have a problem. Obviously, the part with the leaves is more valuable because that's where the bananas grow. Whoever gets that part will have the advantage."

"You're right," Monkey replied. "I'll tell you what. If you let me keep the upper part, I'll give you half of the bananas I **harvest** from it."

"You're very smart and fair to think of such a good solution. I accept your offer."

Monkey took his half away and planted it where Turtle couldn't see it. "Ha, ha! I certainly fooled Turtle!" he thought. "I'll eat all the bananas myself and tell him there weren't any."

As soon as Monkey was out of sight, Turtle planted his half on the riverbank. "Ha, ha! I certainly fooled Monkey," he thought. "I can't wait to see his face when he finds out his half won't live without roots."

Of course, Monkey's half of the banana plant soon **withered** and died in the hot sun. However, Turtle's half grew into a tall tree and produced large bunches of bananas.

Turtle was very happy with his crop. He came every day to see whether the bananas were ripe yet. At last he decided they were ready to pick. But a horrible truth **dawned** on him—he could never pick those bananas. Everyone knows that turtles cannot climb trees.

While Turtle was standing there **grieving**, who should come scampering by but Monkey. When he saw the banana tree, he stopped and stared at it **suspiciously**. "Do you mean to tell me," he said to Turtle, "that your half of the banana plant grew into this?"

"Well . . . yes," answered Turtle, nervously. "And I'm just as surprised as you are. But I'm sure that your half must have twice as many bananas as this does."

"You liar!" said Monkey **indignantly**. "You know as well as I do that I got the bad half. My tree died just a few days after I planted it."

"Oh, what a shame! But I'll tell you what I'll do. I'll give you half of these bananas if you'll pick the whole bunch for me."

Monkey looked up at the ripened yellow fruits. Then he grinned. "All right, I'll do it," he said, and he ran up the tree.

Monkey began to pick the bananas. But instead of bringing them down to Turtle, he stayed up in the tree and ate them. As he finished each one, he threw the peel down to the ground.

Turtle watched without saying anything until Monkey had eaten about half the bunch. Then he called to Monkey, "Stop eating now. The rest are my share."

Monkey peered down at Turtle. "Your share? Why, you're getting your half. Your half is right there at your feet." He pointed at the banana peels on the ground and laughed. Then he tossed down another peel that hit Turtle right in the face.

Turtle was furious. There must be a way to get even with Monkey! As Turtle planned his revenge, he noticed a bush with long, sharp thorns. He went over to the bush, stood on his hind legs, and leaned his hard-shelled back against the prickly branches. When he pushed backward, the branches bent. When he stopped pushing, the branches sprang back, bouncing him forward.

Turtle began to hum as he gently rocked back and forth, back and forth. He said loudly, "Oh, what fun it is to play on this bouncing bush! This is even better than picking bananas!"

Monkey stopped eating and watched Turtle. "I want to play on the bouncing bush too," he said. "I'm going to jump into the bush and see how high it will bounce me."

"No, no!" cried Turtle, as he slipped off the bush. "You're too heavy. You'll wear all the bounce out of my bouncing bush, and it will be spoiled for me."

Monkey ignored Turtle's pleas. "Look out, here I come!" he yelled. Then monkey flung himself into the middle of the bush.

The moment Monkey landed on the bush, a hundred or more sharp-pointed needles stabbed into his back and sides and feet. He screamed in pain and thrashed about **frantically**, trying to get out of the thorny bush. "I'll get you for this, Turtle!" he shouted as he finally staggered free. But Turtle had gone into hiding. He had crawled among some rocks and **retreated** into his shell.

Monkey started pulling the thorns out of his backside. Oh, how those things hurt! Then he sat down on a rock and started pulling thorns out of his feet and legs. While he was doing this, he thought he felt the rock move. But of course that was impossible. Then he felt it again. Either the rock he was sitting on *was* moving, or . . . Aha! Monkey realized that he had just found his missing friend.

"There you are, you **scoundrel**!" Monkey cried, jumping up. "Did you think you could escape from me by hiding in your shell?"

Turtle was shaking with fear. "Friend Monkey, please forgive me! I acted in anger because you cheated me out of my share of bananas."

But Monkey was too mad to listen to Turtle's explanation. He picked up a rock and said, "Enough talk! I'm going to pound you into little pieces with this stone."

At that, Turtle's expression suddenly changed. It went from terror to **smug** self-confidence. "Go ahead," he answered. "Pound me to pieces, and each piece will turn into a new turtle. Please be sure to make lots and lots of pieces. The more turtles, the better."

Monkey was **baffled**. "If I break Turtle into hundreds of pieces," he thought, "the whole island will soon be covered with turtles. That would not be good. I'll have to find another punishment for Turtle."

"Forget the stone," Monkey said. "Instead of pounding you, I will throw you into a fire. I will fan the flames as you beg me for mercy."

Turtle started giggling. "Hee, hee, oh, excuse me," he said. "It's just that fire tickles me. I have a hard shell, so fire doesn't bother me. I only feel a ticklish sensation. Hee, hee, go ahead, it's been quite some time since I had a good laugh."

Again Monkey was **stumped**. "Well, there must be something you're afraid of," he said. "Come on, what is it? Out with it!"

Turtle looked over at the river and then quickly looked away. "Do you think I'm so stupid as to tell you what I fear most? No, I'll never tell you." Then he glanced at the river again and gave a little shiver.

"I know," Monkey cried triumphantly. "You're afraid of the water!"

Turtle started to cry. "I beg you, please," he said, "don't throw me into the river! I can't swim. I will surely sink and drown if you do."

Monkey laughed. "Let this be a lesson to you. Next time think twice before you try to trick me." And with that, he grabbed Turtle and flung him into the river. There was a loud splash, and Turtle disappeared from view.

"Finally, I'm rid of that pest," Monkey said to himself. He turned and began to walk away. Suddenly he heard laughter. He turned back, and to his surprise, he saw Turtle bobbing up and down in the water.

Monkey was **astounded**. "You can swim?" he asked.

"Of course I can," Turtle said. "I am a water creature. I was born in the water, so I feel quite at home in it."

"But you said . . . "

Turtle laughed again and chanted **mockingly**: "Smart the Monkey may be, but still outsmarted is he!"

Then Turtle swam away, leaving Monkey standing frustrated and defeated on the riverbank.

INSIGHTS

The Philippine Islands are located in the Pacific Ocean, southeast of China. Bananas are one of the islands' most important crops. Plantations in the southern islands grow bananas for export throughout the world. Since the banana plant is a means of livelihood for so many people, it's not surprising that it is featured in many Filipino myths, legends, and folktales.

Although it grows to a height of ten to twenty feet, the banana plant is not a tree but an herb. This means that its "trunk" has no woody tissue. It also means that after the plant has borne fruit, it dies. However, a new plant springs up from the underground rootstock of the old plant.

The individual banana fruits are called "fingers," and they grow in clusters called "hands." Five to fifteen hands make up a bunch. Since a bunch may contain from 50 to 150 bananas, it's clear that Monkey must have had a very good appetite.

The character of Monkey appears in many world myths, including Asian stories. He is usually portrayed as a tricky schemer, pleased with his own cleverness and always trying to cheat other animals. Often, however, he is outsmarted by his intended victim. The animal that gets the better of Monkey is sometimes a deer or rabbit and sometimes, as in this story, a turtle.

THE KIND FOOL

VOCABULARY PREVIEW

The following words appear in the story. Review the list and get to know the words before you read the story.

ashen—pale; sickly
bolted—dashed; suddenly ran off
cordially—politely; kindly
despair—sorrow; sadness
dilemma—problem; predicament
gratitude—thanks; appreciation
hoodwinked—tricked; cheated
ineptly—clumsily; poorly
loft—attic; upper room
meekly—shyly; quietly
spare—save; leave alone
wager—challenge; bet

Main Characters

Nakhle-Akhal—foolish man
Hoshiar Khan—Nakhle-Akhal's wise friend

Nakhle-Akhal is not a wise man. Fortunately, he learns a few tricks from his clever friend.

The Kind Fool

Adapted from a tale from India

In an Indian village called Tarka Nagari,[1] there lived a very kind but a very stupid man. His name was Nakhle-Akhal,[2] which means "Mr. Imitation Brains." Everyone in town knew him. They also knew about his mental limitations. So almost everyone cheated him since it was such an easy thing to do.

One day Nakhle-Akhal got lost while looking for the house of an old friend. Although he had walked to the house many times, he couldn't quite remember the way. He made one left turn and two rights when he should have made one right and two lefts. Or was it the other way around? Whatever the case, he ended up in a place where nothing looked familiar.

He saw a group of five boys playing along the road and decided to ask them for help. "My good fellows," he said. "I seem to have lost my way. I am trying to find the house of my old friend Hoshiar Khan.[3] Would you happen to know where he lives?"

[1] (tär´ kä nä gä´ rē)
[2] (nä´ kl ȧk´ hȧl)
[3] (hō´ shər kän)

"If we show you," one of the children asked, "what will you give us in return?"

"My **gratitude**," replied Mr. Imitation Brains, sincerely.

The boys turned and began to walk away.

"Wait. If you help me find my friend's house, I'll buy you some lumps of sweets—the biggest and the best!"

The boy who had asked the question winked at the others. He said to Nakhle-Akhal, "I will accept your offer."

The children pointed to something behind Nakhle-Akhal and told him to turn around. There, directly across the street, was Hoshiar Khan's house!

"Now give us our reward," the boys demanded.

Nakhle-Akhal had made a deal, and the boys did show him the house. So of course he kept his promise. He accompanied the boys to a nearby store and bought each a handful of sweets.

"This is not the biggest lump," one of the boys said. "You promised us the largest lump!"

Nakhle-Akhal took more coins out of his purse and bought more sweets for the children. But again they complained that he hadn't given them the biggest lump. They demanded that he buy more sweets.

Nakhle-Akhal was almost down to his last coin when his friend Hoshiar Khan appeared. Hoshiar Khan had been walking by the store and heard the boys' demands. So he came inside to see what was going on.

Now Hoshiar Khan was known throughout the town for his intelligence and good sense. Even the children of the town looked up to him. Consequently as soon as he reached his friend's side, the five noisy pests suddenly became respectful gentlemen. With great relief in his voice, Nakhle-Akhal explained his **dilemma** to his friend.

Hoshiar Khan gave the boys a look that made them hang their heads. Then he took five sweets of unequal size, showed them to the first boy, and said, "Look here, what are these?"

"Lumps of sweets," the tallest boy said **meekly**.

"Good. Now which one is the biggest lump?"

The same boy pointed to the biggest lump.

"Take it and go. You were promised the biggest lump, and now you have it."

With four pieces left, Hoshiar Khan did the same with the next boy. He did it again with the next, and the next, until only one boy was left. The last boy had no choice but to take the smallest piece since it was the biggest lump left.

"Thank you so much," Nakhle-Akhal said to Hoshiar Khan when the last boy had gone. "Had you not come to my rescue, I would have run out of money."

"You should not be going around town making deals. People tend to take advantage of you."

"Funny that you should say such a thing. Something like that happened on my way to your house. I started my journey this morning with my old horse. He was carrying all my silk merchandise and many other valuable items. As I passed the butcher shop, the owner came out and approached me. He pointed to the horse and asked me how much I would sell it for. I knew my horse was old and weak, yet I named a very high price. Four hundred rupees,[4] I told him. To my surprise, he agreed and immediately handed me four hundred rupees."

"I don't see anything unlucky about that," Hoshiar Khan said.

"Neither did I, until he started to lead my horse away with all my merchandise on it! Of course I tried to stop him. But the butcher said that when he pointed to the horse and asked its price, I didn't say anything about not including the merchandise. How could I argue with that?"

"This man took all you had? He has tricked you!" exclaimed Hoshiar Khan.

"Yes, I have lost all my things. And just now I spent much of my money on candy," said the poor fool.

[4] (rü´pēs) A *rupee* is the paper currency of India. One rupee equals 80 to 90 cents.

"Don't worry, my friend, we'll get your possessions back. I have an idea. Please come into my house."

Hoshiar Khan got out two of the most expensive-looking outfits he owned. He had Nakhle-Akhal put on one outfit, and he put on the other. "Now," he said, "we are ready to play the part of rich men who can buy anything we want. Let us pay a visit to that butcher shop."

When they got to the shop, they were greeted **cordially** by the butcher. After looking around a bit, Hoshiar Khan said, "I'd like to buy some heads."

"Did you say heads?" the butcher said. "Well, you've come to the right place! There's a discount if you buy a large quantity. How many do you want?"

"I'd like to buy all the heads in the store."

The butcher's face lit up, and he began to bark orders to his assistant. He instructed the assistant to quickly gather all the goat heads[5] in the shop and wrap them up well.

When this was done, the butcher presented the package to Hoshiar Khan. "Here you are, all the heads in the store."

Hoshiar Khan frowned. "These are not all the heads. What about yours and your assistant's? Are they not heads? Are they not in the store?"

The butcher's face turned **ashen**. His assistant **bolted** out the door like a frightened mouse.

"Kind sir, I beg you," the butcher said. "Surely when I agreed to sell you all the heads in the store, I did not include my own."

Hoshiar Khan pointed to Nakhle-Akhal and said, "And surely, when my friend here agreed to sell you his horse, he did not mean to include the merchandise on it."

The butcher suddenly recognized Nakhle-Akhal as the man he had **hoodwinked** earlier. He fell on his knees before Nakhle-Akhal and started to cry.

"Please," he said, "**spare** my life! I will return everything I took from you—the horse and all the merchandise."

---

[5] In traditional Indian homes, a goat head is prepared for meals.

"You bought the horse rightfully," Hoshiar Khan said, "so you may keep it. Just return the merchandise that was loaded on it. And lend us the horse long enough to get the merchandise back to my friend's house."

Since his assistant was still hiding, the butcher himself had to load the merchandise onto the horse. Next he called upon his twelve-year-old son to follow the two gentlemen and bring back the horse. Then, bowing and smiling, he thanked Hoshiar Khan and Nakhle-Akhal again and again for their kindness.

As the two friends led the way toward Nakhle-Akhal's house, Hoshiar Khan asked, "By the way, why did you have all of these things with you if you were coming to see me?"

"Heavens, I almost forgot!" Nakhle-Akhal said. "I came with all these goods to ask you if you could help me sell them. They are all I own."

"Why sell everything you own?"

"I lost a **wager** last night. And according to the terms of the bet, after two days the loser must give the winner the first thing the winner touches in the loser's house. Naturally, the winner is going to touch my chest of jewels and precious stones. I have been saving those for my old age, and the thought of losing them fills me with **despair**. So I decided to sell all my other valuables. With the money I make, I can replace my chest of jewels."

Hoshiar Khan smiled. "You need not lose or sell anything, my friend," he said. "This is all you have to do." Then he lowered his voice and spoke several sentences close to his friend's ear.

The next day, Nakhle-Akhal got up early and built a small open **loft** under the roof of his house. He built it in such a way that anyone who wanted to reach it had to climb a ladder. Then he carefully placed his box of jewels and precious stones in the loft. He put it in plain sight. He then draped a cloth over it as if trying to hide it. Finally he removed the ladder and laid it on the floor nearby.

When the winner of the bet came to claim his prize, he immediately saw the loft and the **ineptly** hidden chest in it.

He gave a bitter laugh. "Is that the best you can do? I almost feel guilty doing this!"

He looked around and saw the ladder. He picked it up, placed it against the edge of the loft, and started climbing.

"Stop!" Nakhle-Akhal said.

"Why?" the man said. "I won the bet, and I came to claim my prize."

"Exactly. The ladder was the first thing you touched, and now it is yours. Take it and be gone, for I have just finished my business with you, and you have already overstayed your welcome."

After that, Nakhle-Akhal tried hard to stay out of trouble. He didn't always succeed. But at least he had his good friend Hoshiar Khan to help him when he failed.

INSIGHTS

In Rajasthan,[1] a state in northwestern India, both children and adults love to gather around storytellers. The listeners encourage the storyteller with a soft chant called the *hunkara*.[2] The sound they make is something between a word and a gurgle. It sounds somewhat like "hun hun." They keep the sound low and indistinct, being careful not to distract the storyteller. But the meaning of the chant is clear: "Keep going," the listeners are saying. "We are enjoying your story."

The types of characters in these tales represent groups of people in Indian society. The *Brahman*[3] is a wise man. If a story calls for a priest or a scholar, that character will probably be a Brahman. The *Rajput*[4] is a brave warrior who will risk everything to gain power and glory. The *Bania*[5] is a trader or a banker, very shrewd about money. The *Jat*,[6] a simple but sensible man, earns his living as a farmer. The *Miyan*,[7] a member of the ruling class, is usually portrayed as a cheat and a bungler.

Another popular character, not only in Rajasthan but all over India, is the clever man. Hoshiar Khan, the hero in this story, is an example of this type. In some stories the clever man is kind and good, like Hoshiar Khan. But in others he is a rascal, like Rakhal[8] in a story called "The Cleverest Man in the Kingdom."

In this tale, Rakhal spends his boyhood playing pranks on people and animals. His behavior only gets worse as he grows older. Finally his teachers expel him from school, and his parents disown him.

[1] (rä´ jə stän)
[2] (hun´ kä rä)
[3] (brah´ mun)
[4] (räj´ put)
[5] (bän´ yeh)
[6] (jót)
[7] (mĕ´ yan)
[8] (räk häl´)

But Rakhal is not the least bit sorry. "Just you wait and see," he tells his parents. "The day will come when you'll be proud to claim me as your son."

He travels to a country where the ruler has just made an important announcement. The ruler will give his daughter in marriage to the most clever man in the kingdom. Rakhal makes plans to show that he is that man.

Dressed as a priest, Rakhal tricks the police chief's wife and daughter into giving him all of their jewels. When the king himself rides out to find the robber priest, Rakhal changes his disguise to that of a beggar.

While on the road, he meets the king and tricks the king into exchanging clothes with him. In the king's clothing, Rakhal then rides to the palace and orders the guards, "If a beggar comes here claiming to be the king, put him in prison!"

Later when the guards have discovered their mistake and the king is back on his throne, Rakhal confesses his trickery. In doing so he proves that he is the most clever man in the kingdom. He marries the princess and becomes the crowned prince. When he goes home to visit his parents, they are indeed proud to welcome him.

A·S·I·A·N

HOW AND WHY

Why the Carabao Moves So Slowly

Why Bats Fly at Night

The River of Stars

Why do bats fly at night? Why do carabao travel so slowly? How were the stars created?

These are questions people have asked through the ages. Some of the answers come from mythology.

The three Asian myths in this section not only explain an event of nature but also give insight into the cultures they represent. They reveal the humor and creativity of the storytellers who kept these tales alive. In addition, the stories reveal the human and creative sides of the Asian people.

M·Y·T·H·S

WHY THE CARABAO MOVES SO SLOWLY

VOCABULARY PREVIEW

The following words appear in the story. Review the list and get to know the words before you read the story.

agile—quick; light
appalling—disgusting; awful
conceited—self-centered; having an overly high opinion of oneself
engrossed—involved; absorbed
haughty—stuck-up; snooty
humble—simple; modest
immensely—greatly; beyond measurement
incensed—extremely angered; enraged
smugly—proudly; boastfully
virtues—good qualities

Main Characters

Carabao—beast of burden
Cow—friend of Carabao

Long ago, the carabao was much different from what he is today. He used to be agile, handsome, and reliable. But a harmless swim with his friend changed all that.

Why the Carabao Moves So Slowly

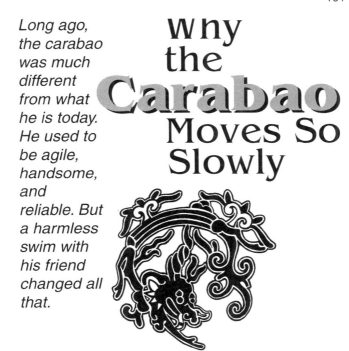

Adapted from a Filipino tale

Most people probably know the carabao that pulls the farmer's plow as a beast of many **virtues**. He is strong, steady, hardworking, obedient, mild-mannered, and patient. But he is also *slo-o-o-w.*

However, he hasn't always been so poky. At one time long ago, the carabao was quite **agile** and quick on his feet. He looked different too. Instead of the black coat he has now, he wore a light brown one. The story of how these changes came about is both sad and funny.

The story begins many years ago in a small village. Each year on May 14, the villages celebrated Carabao[1] Day. Now most animals, if they were honored with such a holiday, might become **conceited**. But Carabao remained

[1] (kar´ ə bau)

humble. When he asked his master, Mang Catalino,[2] for a favor, his words were extremely polite.

"Today is Carabao Day," he said, "and I wonder if I might have your permission to take the day off. I would like to go swimming with my friend Cow."

His master replied, "I can't spare you for the whole day; there is too much work to be done. But you may take the morning off. Just promise me you'll start home when the sun climbs to the middle of the sky."

"I give you my word. I'll start home at noon."

Carabao trotted off happily to his favorite watering hole. His friend Cow was already there, waiting for him. Before they went into the water, they took off their skins, in much the same way that people take off their clothes.

This "undressing" was Cow's idea. She was very proud of her lovely black skin, and she was afraid that it might fade from soaking in water too much. Although Carabao didn't really care what the water did to his skin, he went along with Cow's idea. He admired Cow very much and thought that whatever she did was just right.

"Oh, this feels so good!" Carabao exclaimed as they jumped into the cool, soothing water of the pond. "How wonderful it would be if I could come here all the time!"

"Well, why can't you?" Cow asked.

"Because my master won't let me. He needs me to work all day."

"That's what I've never understood about you," said Cow. "You let your master treat you like a slave. Look how hard he makes you work! You should demand your rights."

"Don't make him sound so bad, my friend," Carabao said. "My master is good to me. Even though I work all day, I don't really mind because he's very kind. He gives me plenty of food, and I have a sturdy shelter from the sun and the rain. When I finish work for the day, he lets me take a dip in a mudhole. Then all my aches and pains disappear."

---

[2] (mang cä tä lē′ no)

Cow was not convinced. "I don't know. I still say your master is taking advantage of you."

"What about you? Surely your master makes you do something to earn your keep."

"*My* master!" said Cow with a toss of her head. "Why, I have no master. I come and go as I please."

"What about that man who sometimes comes to fetch you home? Isn't he your master?"

"Far from it! He is my servant. He feeds me, gives me water, milks me when I ask him to, and leads me to the best pasture he can find. He works hard, and it's all for my benefit."

"You're very lucky," said Carabao.

"Or very smart," said Cow, **smugly**.

The two friends talked on and on, enjoying themselves **immensely**. First they discussed the important issues of the day. One of these was a problem that worried both of them—the overpopulation of flies.

For a while they talked about the weather. Then they gossiped a little about other animals they knew. Cow reported that a whole family of pigs had disappeared from her farm.

"Not that I miss them," Cow immediately added. "Pigs' eating habits are **appalling**, you know."

"Where did they go?"

"They said they were going on vacation," answered Cow. "And they acted very **haughty** because they were riding in a cart. But later I heard my servant say that they were headed for the meat market."

"What's that?" asked Carabao.

"Who knows? Who cares?" answered Cow.

The sun climbed to the top of the sky, but Carabao didn't notice. It slid slowly down the other side, but still Carabao didn't notice. He was too comfortable and too **engrossed** in his conversation with Cow to remember his promise.

Then he heard a voice in the distance and looked up. A man was approaching the pond, calling, "Come, Cow.

Come, Cow."

"There's your servant, Cow. He's walking this way, and he's carrying a stick."

"That's his walking stick," said Cow, without looking around. "He never touches me with it, except to guide me when the path is rough."

"That's good," said Carabao, "because he seems to be rather annoyed."

Hearing this, Cow turned her head. She was just in time to see the man raise the stick and wave it threateningly.

"Oops!" she said. "I guess it's getting late. I'd better be going."

"I guess your servant is a little upset. Perhaps he's forgotten who the master is," said Carabao.

As she splashed through the water, Cow called back, "If my servant is upset, think how **incensed** your master will be."

"Oh, my, it *is* late!" cried Carabao, suddenly realizing that the shadows had grown quite long. "My master will be furious!" He followed Cow out of the water as fast as he could.

Cow, in her haste, grabbed the first skin she saw and put it on. She was so nervous that she didn't even notice that it was brown instead of black. For a moment, she did wonder why it felt so loose. But she had no time to think about this question. Her servant was almost upon her, swinging his stick. Cow took off for home at a run.

Carabao quickly grabbed the remaining skin. He held it up and immediately realized there was a problem.

"Wait, Cow, wait!" bellowed Carabao. "You've got my skin!" But Cow didn't even look back.

Carabao had no choice but to put on Cow's skin. Of course, it was far too small for him. But after several minutes of puffing, snorting, grunting, and groaning, he managed to squeeze himself into it. However, the skin was stretched to its limits. It was so tight that Carabao could hardly move.

He started home, straining with every step. It took him twice as long to cover the distance as it had that morning.

Carabao's master was so angry that he beat Carabao with a stick. From that day on, he refused to let Carabao stay in a shelter anymore. Instead, Carabao was tied to a tree. Worst of all, he never again let Carabao go swimming with Cow. So Carabao never had a chance to get his old skin back.

And that's why Carabao moves so slowly.

INSIGHTS

The carabao, which are also known as the Indian buffalo and the water buffalo, are common in many Asian countries. In most places, carabao are domesticated and used for plowing the rice fields. They are also valued for their milk and their hides.

In the Philippines, the carabao is an essential partner of the farmer. In many farming households, the animal is considered the most valuable of all the family's possessions. Many farmers do not have enough money to buy expensive farming machinery, so they rely solely on the carabao. Generally the estimation of a farmer's wealth is based on the number of carabao he owns.

Many other stories about this animal are told in Asian countries. According to one of them, the carabao was once beautiful. With his long, straight horns proudly sticking out of his head, he was the envy of the other animals. However, he was also disliked because he was lazy and vain and never bathed. The other animals complained about his rude behavior and awful stench, but he told them to mind their own business.

When the king of the animals heard about this, he punished the carabao by sending tigers to attack him. The tigers left him scarred and beaten in a shallow pool of mud.

Today, the carabao is a beast of burden, his punishment for being lazy. Now he is ugly, his punishment for being vain. And he must wallow in mud all day, his punishment for being dirty.

WHY BATS FLY AT NIGHT

VOCABULARY PREVIEW

The following words appear in the story. Review the list and get to know the words before you read the story.

aliases—phony or false names
battalion—military unit
bewildered—puzzled; confused
decree—rule; order
gruffly—harshly; abruptly
nimbly—quickly; easily
perch—roost; seat
rummaged—searched; hunted
scurry—hurry; race
skeptical—doubtful; suspicious
skitter—skip; glide
valiant—brave; gallant
versatile—having many talents; resourceful

Main Characters

the bat—assumes the identity of a bird and a rat
Lam—King of Kosala
captain of the birds—leader of birds
captain of the rats—leader of rats

The bat wasn't always a lonely creature of the night. He once considered himself talented and clever. But he was too clever for his own good. To this day, he still hides in shame.

Why Bats Fly at Night

Inspired by a tale from Laos

Long ago, the bat was very different from the animal we know today. He used to fly in the daytime and **perch** upright anywhere he liked. And he could run on the ground just as easily as he could fly.

"I am so talented and **versatile**," bragged the bat. "No animal is exactly like me." His claims confused the other animals, which pleased the bat very much. In fact, he used their confusion to get the best of both worlds.

Sometimes the bat would soar with a flock of birds and say, "I am a bird!"

Once in a while a **skeptical** bird would say to the bat, "You don't look like one to me. And I ought to know— I've been a bird all my life."

140

But the bat would smugly reply, "What other animals, besides birds, can fly? None! Therefore, any animal that flies as well as I do must be a bird."

No bird could argue with that. So whenever the bat wanted to, he flew with the birds and perched in the trees with them. He also shared their food. Insects, worms, fruits, seeds—whatever the birds ate, he ate too.

When the bat got tired of flying, he would **scurry** around on the ground with the rats. Then he would say, "I'm a rat! I'm a rat!"

A rat might ask, "What makes you think you're one of us? Why don't you take those wings and fly away?"

The bat would answer, "Do you see my teeth? Do you see my fur? No bird has teeth or fur. Besides, who but a rat could **skitter** over the ground as **nimbly** and as boldly as I do?"

No rat could argue with that. So whenever he wanted to, the bat ran with the rats. Like a rat, he **rummaged** for scraps and leftovers. He could make a meal on anything he found.

For a long time the bat enjoyed his double identity. This allowed him to get the best of both worlds. If the birds were taking a vacation, he'd fly south with them. If the rats planned a feast, he'd dine on their food.

Then one day the great King Lam[1] called a meeting of all creatures in his kingdom. He announced that a bridge needed to be built over the ocean from India to the island of Lanka.[2] Lam and his army were at war with the demon king of Lanka. The bridge would help Lam's army attack the enemy. Every creature in the land was expected to help in the construction.

Immediately after the order, the captain of the birds called his winged friends together. "We can't let our king down," commanded the captain. "We must work hard to construct this bridge. Our job will be to bring twigs and grass for the spiders to weave into rope. Each of us must help."

[1] Lam is Rama's name in the Laotian language. Rama is a Hindu god.
[2] (lan´ kə)

With that, all the birds flew off to begin their task. But the bat sat lazily by a tree. He was peacefully munching on seeds when the captain of the birds saw him there.

The captain said **gruffly**, "Why are you not gathering twigs and grass? You will join the rest of the birds to help our **valiant** king."

The bat shook his head. "Sorry captain, can't do it."

"What do you mean, you can't do it?"

"Well, I've been meaning to tell you that I'm not really a bird."

The captain of the birds stared at him. "What do you mean?" he said. "You can fly, can't you? You have always said that any animal that flies as well as you must be a bird."

"But how many birds do you know who have teeth like mine?" he said, opening his mouth. "Or fur like mine?" he said, holding out his arm. "Tell me, how many birds do you know who can run along the ground as nimbly and boldly as I can?" Without waiting for a reply, he turned over to sun his stomach.

The captain of the birds was **bewildered**. He didn't know how to answer the bat's arguments. On the one hand, if only birds can fly, then anything that flies must be a bird. On the other hand, if no bird has teeth and fur, then anything with teeth and fur must not be a bird. It was all so confusing! Without saying another word, the captain flew away.

Just as the captain of the birds flew away, the captain of the rats was leading his busy rat **battalion** past. The captain yelled at the bat. "Maybe you haven't heard, but King Lam needs our help. Every rat will be collecting stones for the bridge."

The bat pretended to be asleep as the rat continued. "You will join the glorious rat battalion that will help King Lam build his bridge. History will record that we rats did more to ensure Lam's victory than all the other animals put together."

The bat paused for a moment, opened one eye, then the other, and said, "Sorry, captain, but I can't join your rat brigade."

"Why not?" asked the captain in surprise.

"I've been waiting for the right moment to break this to you. You see, I'm not really a rat. Therefore, I don't deserve your glory."

"Not a rat? How can that be? You have teeth, don't you?"

"That's right," replied the bat. "Nice, sharp ones," he said, touching the point of each tooth.

"You have fur, don't you?" asked the captain.

"That's right, the furriest," replied the bat as he stroked his hair.

"You can run just like the other rats, can't you?"

"That's right, even faster," said the bat, with a big yawn.

"You have all the characteristics of a rat. You are obviously a rat," the captain declared.

"That's where you're wrong. How many rats do you know who can fly?" asked the bat.

The captain of the rats was silent. He couldn't think of a single rat who could fly. "Well," he said at last, "I guess you don't fit in with us rats after all. How unlucky for you!"

As soon as the captain of the rats was out of earshot, the bat had a good laugh. "What fools," he thought. "There will be no bridge-building for me." With that taken care of, he sat down to have a snack and take a nap.

The captain of the birds and the captain of the rats told Lam of the bat's refusal to help. The news made the king furious!

"How dare he refuse!" Lam thundered. "Every other creature in the land is fulfilling its duty to the king. And this bat escapes by confusing us with **aliases**? This will not go unpunished."

The king quickly scribbled an official note and handed it back to the captains. "Gather every creature of the forest and read this decree. And I mean *every* creature."

A special meeting was called, and all anxiously awaited the message. Only for very special reasons did the king call everyone together. "Please read this, clever monkey," said the captains.

The monkey unrolled the note and read:

"I, King Lam, do **decree** that from this day on, the bat will follow these three rules. Rule number one, the bat is forbidden to fly in the daytime or set foot on the land. He can no longer fly with the birds or run with the rats. Rule number two, since he did not want to be a member of a group, the bat must forever live apart from other animals. Rule number three, since he always turned his stories upside down, depending on whom he was talking to, he must sleep upside down from now on."

All heads turned to see how the bat would respond. In shame, he hung his head and flew away. It was the last time the bat was seen in daylight.

That is why bats fly only at night and sleep by day. That is why they keep to themselves and never mix with the other animals. That is why they sleep upside down in trees, cliffs, and caves. Today, no one would ever mistake a bat for a bird or a rat.

INSIGHTS

This Laotian[1] folktale is from the *Ramayana,*[2] a great epic tale from India. The tales of King Rama and his queen Sita have spread to many other Asian countries, including Indonesia, Thailand, Cambodia, and Laos. Each time part of the tale is told in another country, the new version takes on the values, characteristics, and language of the host culture.

The Ramayana, which the Laotians call *Pha Lak Pha Lam,*[3] is a series of episodes about the life of the heroic King Rama. It also includes lessons on how to behave, what to believe in, and why certain things came to be. The part of the story retold in this book explains why the bat is a *nocturnal,* or a night, creature. King Lam (the name for King Rama in the Laotian version) is in the story, but the tale centers around the antics of the bat.

In another part of *Pha Lak Pha Lam*, Lam's queen Sida is kidnapped. She is being held on the island of Lanka (present-day Sri Lanka). In order to get his army across the strait[4] separating India and Lanka, Lam needs to build a bridge. But the King of the Ocean refuses to cooperate—bridges are against his principles. He says, "You know that every element has its own inherent qualities. Mine are to be deep and hard to cross."

However, the King of the Ocean gives Lam some advice. He advises Lam to hire a monkey named Nala,[5] who has the power to make stones float. Lam does so, and with the help of the monkey, the bridge is built.

---

[1] (la′ ō shən)
[2] (rä′ mə yä na)
[3] (pä läk pä läm)
[4] A *strait* is a narrow passageway of water connecting two larger bodies of water. The strait between India and Sri Lanka is 33 miles wide.
[5] (nü lü)

THE RIVER OF STARS

VOCABULARY PREVIEW

The following words appear in the story. Review the list and get to know the words before you read the story.

affection—liking; love
consequently—as a result; so
defy—disobey; ignore
descended—moved downward; landed
fetched—got; went for
glistened—glittered; sparkled
instantly—at once; right away
iridescent—pearly; shiny
loom—frame for weaving thread
meager—small; lowly
mortal—human
scanned—quickly checked; searched
stalk—stem; trunk
startled—frightened; surprised
tan—process that turns animal hide to leather
tapestries—heavy hand-woven fabrics with beautiful designs and images

Main Characters

Cowherd—younger brother
the cow—Cowherd's friend
Weaving Maid—a fairy
Fairy Goddess—Weaving Maid's grandmother

Have you ever wondered how the Milky Way was made? It's a sad story of two lovers who remain worlds apart to this day.

The River of Stars

Adapted from a Chinese folktale

Many, many years ago, an unfortunate boy lived in China. Both of his parents died when he was a small child, leaving the boy and his older brother alone. It was customary for Chinese people to care for their relatives. **Consequently,** the boy's older brother and his wife had to raise the boy.

However, the brother was not kind to the boy. The boy had to sleep on the kitchen floor. His brother gave him only a few pieces of ragged clothes and fed him only a small bowl of rice each day. In return for this **meager** care, the boy had to work very hard. He swept the floor and **fetched** wood for the fire. He also tended the family's vegetable garden. Most importantly, he watched over the family's only cow. For this reason, everyone called the boy Cowherd.

Cowherd was a lonely boy. He usually had no time to play. When he did have the time, none of the village boys paid any attention to him. Even his brother ignored him. But this was better than the way his sister-in-law treated him. She constantly scolded him, saying, "Get up, you lazy thing. Work a little for the rice you eat!"

Cowherd spent his days doing one chore after another. His only friend was the brown and white cow. Each afternoon, Cowherd would take the cow to pasture. He'd find her a spot beneath a tree, out of the hot sun. While she ate the tender grass, he would sit next to her and scratch her soft ears.

"I'm glad you're here," he often said. "You're the only creature in the world who loves me."

The cow would look at him with her velvety brown eyes and moo softly. Cowherd told her all his troubles, and she seemed to understand.

Years passed and the boy's situation didn't improve. One morning, Cowherd's brother left on a trip to the city. His sister-in-law came into the kitchen where Cowherd was preparing breakfast. But for once, she didn't have a long list of chores for him to do.

"Do you know what day it is?" she asked.

Cowherd thought for a moment. It was not planting day. It was not time to harvest rice. It was not New Year's Day or any other holiday.

"I'm sorry, my sister, but I do not know."

"Today is your birthday, Cowherd," his sister-in-law snapped back. "You are eighteen years old. Your brother and I have cared for you since you were eight. You have eaten our food and slept under our roof, doing nothing in return."

Cowherd knew that was not true, but he did not respond.

"You are a grown man now," his sister-in-law continued. "It is time for you to make your own way in the world. By tomorrow morning, I want you out of my house—forever!"

Cowherd could not believe his ears. He knew his brother and sister-in-law had no **affection** for him. But how could they throw him out?

"What am I to do?" he asked sadly. "I won't even have a place to lay my head."

His sister-in-law heard the sadness in his voice and felt a bit guilty. Deep down, she knew the boy had worked hard over the last ten years. "I suppose you can take the cow with you," she said. "It's old, and it hardly gives milk anymore. My husband is buying a younger cow in the city. Maybe you can sell the old cow for a few coins."

Cowherd accepted the offer. He spent the day packing the few rags he had and finishing up odd jobs.

The next morning he went to the barn and slipped a rope of braided grass around his cow's neck. "My sister-in-law told me to sell you," he said to the cow. "But I won't. You come with me. Whatever happens, I'll always take care of you."

The cow mooed and seemed to nod her head. Together they left the yard and began to walk. Cowherd had no idea where to go. He finally led the cow to her favorite pasture. There was a small stream running through the grass, and a few trees provided some shade.

"At least you will have something to eat, old friend," Cowherd said. Then he gathered dry branches and made himself a bed. His cow lay down next to him and kept him warm all night.

As the days went by, Cowherd and his cow remained by the stream. Cowherd built a shelter from branches and grass. He ate fish caught from the stream, and he picked delicious fruits and berries from the trees. The cow grazed peacefully in the pasture and even provided milk for the young man. Both were content.

One evening Cowherd looked up at the stars. His cow lay beside him in the grass. "I am content with my life, but I long for a human companion," he said, looking into the sky. "I often find myself wishing for a wife."

Suddenly, he heard a voice.

"Cowherd."

He looked around. No one was there. His cow stood and chewed her cud.

"I must be hearing things," he murmured, turning his eyes to the stars again.

"Cowherd!" said the voice even louder.

He **scanned** the area, but still no one was there.

"It's me," the cow said. "I want to talk to you."

Cowherd was amazed. "I didn't know cows could talk."

"We only talk when we have something important to say," the cow replied. "Listen carefully. Tomorrow morning, a beautiful fairy named Weaving Maid will bathe in this stream with her sisters. This young maiden will become your wife."

"How will I know which one she is?" asked Cowherd.

"A delicate strand of thread follows her as she flies," answered the cow. She continued, "Now before she goes into the water, she will take off her pink **iridescent** wings. You must take those wings and keep them until she promises to marry you. If you do this, I guarantee you will be a happy and wealthy man. Do you understand?"

"I guess so," Cowherd said. "But . . . "

"No buts," the cow said. "Do as I tell you, and all will be well."

The next morning, Cowherd got up as soon as the sun rose. He washed his face and combed his hair. Then he headed to the stream. Hiding behind a large rock, he waited patiently.

Soon he heard the distant voices of Weaving Maid and her sisters. They swooped down from the sky. Their pink wings sparkled with every color of the rainbow. A silvery powder fell from them as they gently **descended**.

Each one took off her wings and bathed in the cool water. Cowherd was dazzled. Weaving Maid was the most beautiful creature he'd ever seen. He fell in love **instantly**. Stepping out from behind the rock, he gently picked up her delicate pink wings.

One by one, the fairies came out of the water. Each picked up her wings and flew away. Weaving Maid was the last one out. She searched the bank where she had left her wings but found nothing.

"Wait," she called. "Sisters, wait! Don't leave me. I can't find my wings!"

But the other fairies didn't hear her, and they quickly flew off. Weaving Maid sat next to the stream and began to cry.

Cowherd stepped out from behind the rock. "Please don't cry. I know where your wings are. I took them," Cowherd said. He held up her wings, and they **glistened** in the early morning sunlight. "They are almost as beautiful as you."

The **startled** Weaving Maid tried to hide behind a bamboo **stalk**.

"Don't be afraid," Cowherd said. "I'll give them back if you promise to listen to what I have to say."

Weaving Maid didn't respond at first. But the young man seemed kind, so she nodded and agreed, "All right, I'll listen."

"Last night," he said, "my cow spoke to me. She told me you would be here."

Weaving Maid listened as Cowherd told his story. "I was supposed to hold on to your wings until you promised to marry me," he said. "But I don't want you to become my wife because I threatened you. So I'll give you back your wings and ask again."

Somehow he found the courage to say, "I fell in love with you the moment I saw you. Will you marry me?"

"You are so kind and handsome. Your sweet words have touched me," Weaving Maid said, looking into his eyes.

"Then you'll be my wife?" Cowherd asked with hope in his voice.

"If only I could. I am forbidden to marry a **mortal,**" said Weaving Maid, in a saddened voice. "If my grandmother, the Fairy Goddess, found out, I would surely be punished. She would take me far away from you."

"I would hate for you to be punished," said Cowherd as he helped her put on the wings. "I understand."

Cowherd turned to leave when suddenly Weaving Maid said, "Wait! I, too, am overcome by love. If it is still your wish, I will be your wife." So in a small, secret ceremony, the two were married.

Cowherd worked hard to please his wife. He built her a room where she could set her **loom.** Weaving Maid created beautiful **tapestries,** which Cowherd sold in the village for a high price. Working together the two made a good living. Eventually they had two children, a boy and a girl.

Despite her happy life, Weaving Maid was afraid that her grandmother would discover that she had married a human. But the years passed and nothing happened.

One day Cowherd noticed that his faithful cow had grown old. Her legs trembled when she walked, and her coat was thin.

"My friend," Cowherd said aloud. "You do not look well. What can I do to help you?"

The cow spoke again for the first time in many years. "You have already done more for me than any other human. But I'm going to die soon, and I want to leave you a gift for your kindness. After I die, remove my skin and **tan** it so it remains soft. If you are ever in trouble, wrap yourself in my hide, and I will help you."

"I will remember, old friend. You will be missed," Cowherd said.

Soon after, the cow died. Cowherd prepared her coat as she had instructed.

One morning several years later, Fairy Goddess was counting her granddaughters.

"One of you is missing," she announced in an annoyed voice. "Where is Weaving Maid?"

The fairies looked at each other. Finally the bravest spoke up, "I . . . I think she is still on Earth, my grandmother. She did not come back with us one morning when we bathed in the stream."

"Well," Fairy Goddess said, "I'll see about that!"

She swept down toward the earth and looked for her granddaughter. Soon she spotted the home Cowherd had built. A beautifully woven rug was hanging outside. It blended each color of the rainbow with a golden thread. Immediately she thought to herself, "That is the work of Weaving Maid."

Weaving Maid was preparing dinner for their children. Suddenly the walls shook and the windows blew open.

"You disobeyed me!" said the frowning Fairy Goddess as she stood in the doorway.

"I can explain, Fairy Goddess," said Weaving Maid boldly.

"And believe me, you'll have lots of time to explain," said Fairy Goddess, grabbing Weaving Maid. "You are coming home."

"I must stay here. I have to care for my children," Weaving Maid protested, gathering her son and daughter under her arms.

Fairy Goddess pulled her away from the children. "You have no choice," she said. Without saying another word or waiting for a reply, Fairy Goddess grabbed Weaving Maid and flew away.

When Cowherd came home from the fields, he found his children weeping. They told him what had happened.

"I was afraid of this," he said sadly. "Your mother warned me that one day her grandmother might take her away." He sat down with a child on each knee. "Don't cry, little ones. I will think of something, and we'll get her back."

Suddenly Cowherd remembered the cow's skin. Cowherd had given it a place of honor on a wall of their home. Now it was time to put it to use as his friend had instructed him. He grabbed it off the wall and wrapped it around himself and his children. Then he said, "My friend in death, my friend in life. Take me now to find my wife."

Cowherd felt himself rising into the air. He was lifted out of the house and into the sky. He held his children close as he rose higher and higher into the clouds. Soon he reached the home of Fairy Goddess.

Fairy Goddess and Weaving Maid happened to be standing outside when the goddess saw Cowherd coming. She alerted her strongest soldiers to hold Weaving Maid tightly. Then Fairy Goddess pulled a jade pin from her hair. Waving it in the air, a river of silver stars streamed from her hand. As Cowherd approached his wife, the river of stars came between the two lovers. They stood looking longingly at each other.

"Ha, ha!" laughed Fairy Goddess. "You are no match for me, mortal. Go back to Earth, and leave my granddaughter alone!"

But Cowherd would not give up. He wrapped the tanned hide even tighter around him and the children. He chanted, "My friend in death, my friend in life. Please build a bridge to my dear wife."

Suddenly there was the sound of wings. A flock of kindly magpies flew toward Cowherd and Weaving Maid. They formed a bridge across the river of stars. Weaving Maid pulled away from the soldiers. Crying with joy, she ran across the bridge and hugged her husband and children.

"You shall not have her," screamed Fairy Goddess. "No mortal can **defy** me." Fairy Goddess waved her arms, and the magpies quickly parted.

But Weaving Maid stepped in front of her husband and children. "We love each other, and I am happy with him. Don't you want me to be happy? Look at your great-grandchildren. They need the love of both parents. And they need your love too."

As Fairy Goddess listened to Weaving Maid's words, she began to understand her granddaughter's strong feelings of love.

"I can see you will never be happy without your mortal husband," she said to Weaving Maid. "So I have decided to allow him and your children to stay up here. But no mortals may live in the Fairy Kingdom. However, each year on the seventh day of the seventh month, I'll let you visit them." And so it was arranged.

The silver river of stars is still in the sky. We call it the Milky Way.[1] On a clear night, you will see two bright stars,[2] one on each side of the Milky Way. Occasionally, they move closer to each other. These stars are Cowherd and Weaving Maid making another journey to see each other.

---

[1] The Milky Way is Earth's galaxy.
[2] The bright stars are probably Deneb and the planet Jupiter. Jupiter changes location in the sky.

INSIGHTS

"The River of Stars" reflects the traditional Chinese culture. In this lifestyle, the family is the most important part of a person's life. A family is more than just a father, mother, and children. In many families, three or more generations live under the same roof. When a man marries, he and his wife live with his parents.

The oldest male in the household is head of the family. And his word is law. He can order one son to go to school and another to work on the family farm. He can even choose his children's marriage partners. He can also sell the family homestead and move everyone to another city.

However, he is obliged to provide food, clothing, and shelter to every family member, even distant cousins. In the story, Cowherd's sister-in-law makes him leave the family home. That most likely would not happen among traditional Chinese people.

Weaving Maid represents two important features of the traditional Chinese culture. Ancient Chinese people believed that the heavens were full of supernatural creatures. They believed in gods, goddesses, angels, fairies, and spirits. Weaving Maid and her family reflect these beliefs.

Weaving Maid sews beautiful tapestries. Weaving was an important task in every Chinese household. In fact, the most famous weaver in China was the empress Hsi-Ling-Shi.[1]

According to legend, she found strange white worms eating the leaves of the mulberry trees in her garden. She tried to pick the worms' cocoons off the trees so they wouldn't hatch and eat more leaves. One of the cocoons fell into a bucket of hot water. The empress discovered

[1] (shē lin shī)

that the unwound cocoon produced a beautiful, soft thread. She spun the thread and wove it into cloth. This cloth became known as silk. For more than three thousand years, the Chinese were the only people in the world who knew how to make silk. Women produced most of the cloth, and every household had one or more silk weavers.

The marriage between Cowherd and Weaving Maid would have been unusual. A more typical form of matrimony in the culture was arranged or contracted. A father would arrange his child's marriage. He could force a child into a marriage or prevent a marriage from occurring. Few people married for love, as Cowherd and Weaving Maid did.